The Princeton Review®

Math Workout for the SAT

By Cornelia Cooke

THIRD EDITION
RANDOM HOUSE, INC.
NEW YORK

www.PrincetonReview.com

The Independent Education Consultants Association recognizes The Princeton Review as a valuable resource for high school and college students applying to college and graduate school.

The Princeton Review, Inc.
111 Speen Street, Suite 550
Framingham, MA 01701
E-mail: editorialsupport@review.com

ISBN: 978-0-375-42833-3
ISSN: 1551-6431

Editor: Liz Rutzel
Updated by: David Stoll
Production Editor: Michael Mazzei
Production Coordinator: Deborah A. Silvestrini

Manufactured in the United States of America on partially recycled paper.

9 8 7 6 5 4 3 2 1

Third Edition

ACKNOWLEDGMENTS

I would like to thank Chris Kensler, Kristin Fayne-Mulroy, Laurice Pearson, Jane Lacher, Jeannie Yoon, Meher Khambata, and Andrea Gordon for their invaluable help, editing skills, and overall perspicacity. Special thanks to Doug Pierce, Allegra Viner, Patricia Dublin, Stephanie Martin, and Ellen Mendlow. For additional production and editing help, thanks to Andrea Paykin, Andy Lutz, Lee Elliott, Cynthia Brantley, Julian Ham, Peter Jung, Andrew Dunn, Clayton Harding, Kathleen Standard, Jefferson Nichols, Sara Kane, Ramsey Silberberg, Matthew Clark, Dinica Quesada, Carol Slominski, Christopher D. Scott, and Maria Dente. Special thanks also to Christine Parker and the Diagpalooza team.

Special thanks to Adam Robinson, who conceived of and perfected the Joe Bloggs approach to standardized tests and many of the other successful techniques used by The Princeton Review.

CONTENTS

Introduction

IN THE BEGINNING . . .

Even though the SAT is designed for juniors and seniors, most of the math on the test bears little resemblance to the type of math found in the high school classroom. Many students find it hard to believe—not to mention a little humiliating—that a test that seems so difficult actually tests little more than basic algebra, arithmetic, and geometry. Even students who are very good at math in school often have trouble on the SAT. Why?

The fact is that while the SAT uses basic mathematical concepts, it's unlike any math test you will ever see in school. The SAT uses basic math problems in very particular ways. This is why preparing for the SAT requires a new set of skills. The SAT does not test how smart you are, how well you will do in school, or what kind of person you are. It only tests *how well you do on the SAT*. And doing well on the SAT is a skill that can be learned.

How can you improve your score on the SAT? First, you need to learn the structure of the test. This will help you develop an overall test-taking strategy. Then you need to learn some powerful test-taking skills, which will help you think your way through SAT-type problems.

Some of our advice may sound a little strange. In fact, if you try some of our techniques in math class, your teacher will probably be unhappy. But remember: This isn't math class. This is the SAT, and it's your job to get as good at SAT math as you can.

STRUCTURE OF THE MATH SECTIONS

Of the eight scored multiple-choice sections on the SAT, three of them will be math. The questions will be presented in two different formats: regular multiple choice and grid-ins. We will discuss how to deal with each of these question formats.

How to Use this Book

This book is designed for students who want concentrated math preparation. It can be used alone or as a supplement to our *Cracking the SAT*. While we will briefly review the essential Princeton Review test-taking strategies and problem-solving skills. If you want an in-depth guide to these techniques, you'll want to also read *Cracking the SAT*.

Where Does the SAT Come From?

The SAT is published by the Educational Testing Service (ETS) under the sponsorship of the College Entrance Examination Board (the College Board). ETS and the College Board are both private companies. We'll tell you more about them in Chapter 1.

WHAT IS THE PRINCETON REVIEW?

The Princeton Review is one of the nation's premier test-preparation companies. We have conducted courses in hundreds of locations around the country, and we prepare more students for the SAT than anyone else. We also prepare students for the PSAT/NMSQT, ACT, GRE, GMAT, LSAT, MCAT, and other standardized tests.

The Princeton Review's techniques are unique and powerful. We developed them after spending countless hours scrutinizing real SATs, analyzing them with computers, and proving our theories with real students.

This book is based on our extensive experience in the classroom. Our techniques for cracking the SAT will help you improve your SAT scores by teaching you to:

1. think like the test writers at ETS

2. take full advantage of the limited time allowed

3. find the answers to questions you don't understand by guessing intelligently

4. avoid the traps that ETS has laid for you (and use those traps to your advantage)

1
Strategies

We'll say it again: This isn't the kind of test you get in math class. You need some special techniques for handling SAT problems—techniques that will help you go faster and that take advantage of the format of the questions. Some of the things we suggest may seem awkward at first, so practice them. If you do the math questions on the SAT the way your math teacher taught you, you waste time and throw away points.

ORDER OF DIFFICULTY

To formulate an overall test-taking strategy, the most important thing to learn is the order of difficulty of the math sections. The questions on your SAT are selected with extreme care, in the same way, every time. Knowing how the test is put together is crucial for scoring well. The chart on the next page shows you how the questions are organized on each of the math sections.

As you can see, sections are arranged in order of difficulty, with the easy questions at the beginning, medium questions in the middle, and the hard questions at the end of each section. It is crucial to know the difficulty of a question in order to know the best way to solve it. This is so important that the exercises in this book provide an easy, a medium, and a hard question for each major question type. We've kept the question numbers consistent to help you learn which questions are easy, medium, and hard.

JOE BLOGGS

Joe Bloggs is our name for the average SAT tester. Joe isn't stupid—he's just average. He takes this test as he would take a math test in school, and he gets an average score. If you learn how Joe takes this test, you can learn how to take it better.

When Joe takes the SAT, he makes two important mistakes. First, he tries to finish the test. This encourages him to rush through the easy problems, which he should get right, but he makes silly mistakes because he's rushing. He rushes all the way into the hard problems, getting almost no questions right. Why? Because of Joe's second mistake: He thinks that he can solve every problem in a straight-forward way. While this works on the easy problems, the hard problems are full of trap answers, which cause Joe to spend too much time on each question or pick the wrong choice.

How can you avoid being like Joe? First, learn to do the right number of problems. Second, learn some test-taking techniques that will make harder problems much easier and help you avoid the traps that the test writers have laid for you.

PACING

Almost everybody works too fast on the SAT, losing a lot of points due to careless errors. The SAT isn't your usual math situation—you don't get *partial credit* for "having the right idea." The only thing that matters is what you bubble in on your answer sheet. Slow down! If you find yourself making careless mistakes, you are throwing points out the window.

Unless you're shooting for a score of 700 or above, do not finish the math sections. Again, this isn't like math class. The test isn't designed for you to finish, and you'll hurt your score by trying to do so. If you miss a total of around five or six questions for all three sections, you're probably hitting the right pace. More mistakes than that, and you're going too quickly. If you aren't missing any questions but aren't finishing, you should guess more aggressively and try to work a bit faster.

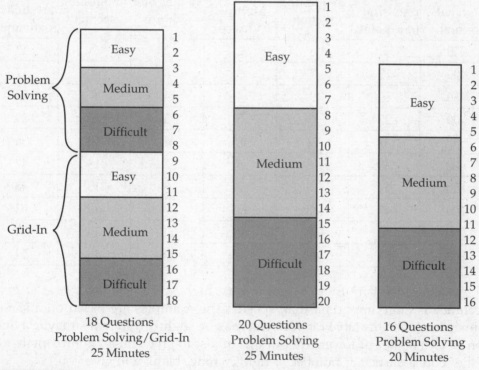

18 Questions
Problem Solving/Grid-In
25 Minutes

20 Questions
Problem Solving
25 Minutes

16 Questions
Problem Solving
20 Minutes

SCORING

If you were betting your hard-earned cash, wouldn't you want to know the odds? On the SAT, you're betting for more points, and it's important to understand how the scoring works so you'll play smart.

For each right answer, you earn one raw point. For each wrong answer, you lose one-quarter of a raw point. That's it. If you leave a question blank, nothing happens either way, except that the total number of points you can earn is reduced.

Every right answer earns you one point, whether it's easy or hard.

That's important to understand, because most people spend too much time on hard questions. They aren't going to do anything more for you than easy questions—and you'll hurt your score if you miss easy or medium questions because you're rushing to finish.

Based on a sample conversion table, here are some examples of what you have to do to get a particular score—there are a total of 54 math questions.

To get (scaled score)	You need to earn: (raw points)	Attempt this many questions				Total # of questions to attempt
		20-question section	8-question Multiple Choice	10-question Grid-Ins	16-question section	
350	7	6	2	2	2	12
400	12	7	3	3	4	17
450	19	9	4	4	6	23
500	25	11	5	5	8	29
550	32	14	6	6	10	36
600	38	16	6	7	13	42
650	44	18	7	8	15	48
700	47	all	all	9	all	53
750	52	all	all	all	all	54
800	54	all	all	all	all	54

Amazing, isn't it? Even to get a very high score, *you don't have to finish.* Accuracy is more important than speed! (The examples are based on a sample conversion table; the table for your test may be slightly different—maybe a question or two higher or lower. We put this in just to give you an approximate idea of the score a particular number of right/wrong/blank will give you.)

GUESSING

Say you start to work on a problem and get stuck. Should you just move on? Not if you can cross out any of the wrong answer choices. Are you working on a hard problem? Then cross out any too-good-to-be-true answers and guess from what's left. Are you working on an easy question? Go with your instincts.

If you can eliminate even one answer choice, guess.

Why? Because if you guessed randomly on five questions, without eliminating anything (let your pet monkey pick the answer), you'd have a one out of five chance of picking a right answer. That one right answer earns you (or your pet monkey) one raw point, and the four wrong answers cost you $4 \times \frac{1}{4}$ of a point subtracted. You break even. Eliminating one or more answer choices improves your odds considerably—so take advantage of it!

WHEN TO GUESS

All of that said, we don't mean to suggest that you skip merrily through the sections guessing with abandon. There are smart places to guess and not-so-smart places to guess.

Always be aware of where you are in the section. Use the order-of-difficulty information to guide your guessing: easy questions = easy answers; hard questions = hard answers.

GOOD GUESS

- Geometry, drawn to scale. If you can approximate the length or area or angle measurement, go for it. Applies to easy, medium, and hard questions.

- Any grid-in you've got an answer for. No penalty for wrong answers.

BAD GUESS

- Too-good-to-be-true answers on hard questions

- Long, complicated word problems at the end of the section. (Spend your time on something shorter and more manageable.)

- Questions you don't have time to read.

CALCULATORS

Seems like a good deal, doesn't it? Well, maybe. It depends on the problem. Don't grab your calculator too quickly—you have to know how solve the problem first.

> **Calculators can only calculate; they can't think. You need to figure out how to solve the problem before you can begin calculating.**

Calculators are great for helping you avoid silly mistakes in your arithmetic, and you should use them when you can. They can help ensure that you make correct calculations, but they can't tell you which calculations are the right ones to make. So be sure you figure out how to solve the problem before you start punching numbers into your calculator.

> **Think before you punch.**

TIPS TO CALCULATOR HAPPINESS

- Get a calculator that follows the order of operations and has keys for x^2, y^x, and $\sqrt{}$.

- Use the same calculator every time you practice SAT problems.

- Check each number after you punch it in.

CARELESS MISTAKES

If you are prone to careless mistakes—and most of us are—you probably make the same kinds of careless mistakes over and over. If you take the time to analyze the questions you get wrong, you will discover which kinds are your personal favorites. Then you can compensate for them when you take the SAT.

In the world, and in math class, it's most important for you to understand concepts and ways to solve problems. On the SAT, it's most important that you bubble in the correct answer. Students typically lose anywhere from 30 to 100 points simply by making careless, preventable mistakes.

Some common mistakes to watch for:

- misreading the question

- computation error

- punching in the wrong thing on the calculator

- on a medium or hard question, stopping after one or two steps, when the question requires three or four steps

- answering a different question from the one asked

If, for example, you find you keep missing questions because you multiply wrong, then do every multiplication twice. Do every step on paper, not in your head. If you make a lot of mistakes on positive/negative, write out each step, and be extra careful on those questions. Correcting careless mistakes is an easy way to pick up more points, so make sure you analyze your mistakes so you know what to look out for.

PLUGGING IN

One of the most powerful math techniques on the SAT is called Plugging In. The idea of Plugging In is to take all of the variables—things like x, y, z—in a problem and replace them with actual numbers. This turns your algebra problems into simple arithmetic and can make even the hardest problem into an easy one.

HOW TO RECOGNIZE A PLUGGING-IN QUESTION

- There are variables in the answer choices.

- The question says something like *in terms of x*.

- Your first thought is to write an equation.

- The question asks for a percentage or fractional part of something, but doesn't give you any actual amounts.

HOW TO SOLVE A PLUGGING-IN QUESTION

- Don't write an equation.

- Pick an easy number and substitute it for the variable.

- Work the problem through and get an answer. Circle it so you don't lose track of it.

- Plug in your number—the one you chose in the beginning—to the answer choices and see which choice produces your circled answer.

Here's an example:

Jill spent x dollars on pet toys and 12 dollars on socks. If the amount Jill spent was twice the amount she earns each week, how much does Jill earn each week in terms of x ?

(A) $2(x + 12)$

(B) $2x + 24$

(C) $\dfrac{x}{2} + 12$

(D) $\dfrac{x+12}{2}$

(E) $\dfrac{x-12}{2}$

Solution: Plug in 100 for x. That means Jill spent a total of 112 dollars. If that was twice her weekly salary, then she makes half of 112, or 56 dollars a week. Circle 56. Now plug 100 into the answers to see which one yields 56.

(A) 2(100 + 12) = 224. No good. (B) is 224, which is also too big. (C) 50 + 12 = 62 (D) $\frac{112}{2}$ = 56! Yes! (E) is $\frac{88}{2}$ = 44. Nope. The answer is (D).

Here's a harder example:

> Karl bought x bags of red marbles for y dollars per bag, and z bags of blue marbles for $3y$ dollars per bag. If he bought twice as many bags of blue marbles as red marbles, then in terms of y, what was the average cost, in dollars, per bag of marbles?
>
> (A) $\frac{3y}{2}$
>
> (B) $\frac{7y}{3}$
>
> (C) $3y - y$
>
> (D) $2y$
>
> (E) $6y$

Solution: You don't really want to do the algebra, do you? Use simple, low numbers and plug in. How about $x = 2$ and $y = 3$? That's 2 bags of red marbles at $3 each. So he spent $6 on red marbles. (In word problems, it helps to keep track of what the numbers represent.) If he bought twice as many bags of blue marbles, then $z = 4$. So he bought 4 bags of blue marbles at $3y$ or $9 a can and spent a total of $36. Now you figure the average price by adding up the dollars spent and dividing that by the total number of bags. He spent $6 + $36 = $42 on 2 + 4 = 6 bags of marbles. So the average price per bag is $\frac{42}{6}$ = $7. Circle $7.

Now, plug 3 in for y in the answer choices and see which one gives you 7. (A) yields $\frac{9}{2}$, so eliminate it. (B) is 7, so that's the answer. The remaining choices are wrong, as well.

Here's a different kind of example:

> At his bake sale, Mr. Heftwhistle sold 30% of
> his pies to one friend. Mr. Heftwhistle then
> sold 60% of the remaining pies to another
> friend. What percent of his original number of
> pies did Mr. Heftwhistle have left?
>
> (A) 10%
> (B) 18%
> (C) 28%
> (D) 36%
> (E) 40%

Solution: If you don't plug in, you may make the sad mistake of picking (A) or of working with ugly fractions. Plugging in a number is much easier. Let's say Mr. Heftwhistle had 100 pies. 30% of 100 equals 30, so he's left with 70. 60% of 70 equals 42, so he's left with 28. Here's the great thing about plugging in 100 on percentage problems—28 (left) out of 100 (original number) is simply 28%. That's it. (C) is the answer.

TIPS FOR PLUGGING IN HAPPINESS

- Pick easy numbers like 2, 4, 10, 100. The best number to choose depends on the question: Use 100 for percents.

- Avoid picking 0, 1, or any number that shows up in the answer choices.

- If the number you picked leads to ugly computations—fractions, negatives, or anything you need a calculator for—bail out and pick an easier number.

- Practice!

On the next page is a Quick Quiz, so you can practice Plugging In before you continue. The question number corresponds to the difficulty level in the 20-question multiple-choice section. Answers and explanations immediately follow every Quick Quiz.

QUICK QUIZ #1

EASY

6. If p is an odd integer, which of the following must also be an odd integer?

   (A) $p + 1$

   (B) $\dfrac{p}{2}$

   (C) $p + 2$

   (D) $2p$

   (E) $p - 1$

MEDIUM

13. If $\dfrac{y}{3} = 6x$, then in terms of y, $x =$

    (A) $3y$

    (B) $2y$

    (C) y

    (D) $\dfrac{y}{2}$

    (E) $\dfrac{y}{18}$

HARD

18. Mary spilled $\dfrac{2}{5}$ of her peanuts, and Jessica ate $\dfrac{1}{3}$ of what was left. Jessica then gave the remaining peanuts to Max and Sam, who each ate half of what remained. What fractional part of Mary's peanuts did Sam eat?

    (A) $\dfrac{1}{15}$

    (B) $\dfrac{1}{10}$

    (C) $\dfrac{1}{5}$

    (D) $\dfrac{1}{3}$

    (E) $\dfrac{4}{5}$

6. **C** Because p has to be odd, make it 3. Try that in the answer choices, and cross out anything that isn't odd. (A): 3 + 1 = 4. Cross out (A). (B): $\frac{3}{2}$. Cross out (B). (Fractions can't be odd or even.) (C): 3 + 2 = 5, leave (C) in. (D): 2(3) = 6. Cross out (D). (E): 3 − 1 = 2. Cross out (E). Only (C) works.

13. **E** Plug in $y = 36$, which makes $x = 2$. Now plug in 36 for y in the answer choices and look for x, which is 2. (A): something huge. (B): still something huge. (C): 36. (D): $\frac{36}{2}$ = 18, still too big. (E): $\frac{36}{18}$ = 2, so (E) is correct.

18. **C** On this kind of question, there aren't variables in the answer choices, but there's an *implied* variable in the question because you don't know how many peanuts Mary started with. Let's say she had 15 peanuts, because the denominators in the fractions are both factors of 15. If she spilled $\frac{2}{5}$ of 15, she spilled 6, leaving her with 9. If Jessica ate $\frac{1}{3}$ of 9, she ate 3, leaving Mary with 6. If Max and Sam split 6, they each ate 3. The fractional part is $\frac{\text{part}}{\text{whole}}$, so Sam's fractional part is $\frac{3}{15}$ or $\frac{1}{5}$. (Whew.)

A tree diagram makes this easier to deal with:

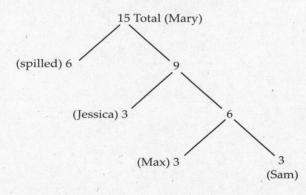

In question 13, you may have had a hard time coming up with numbers that worked evenly. That's OK—it takes practice. You can plug in any numbers you want, as long as they satisfy the conditions of the problem, so you might as well plug in numbers that are easy to work with.

In question 18, you could solve this without plugging in, but then you're dealing with fractional parts of a whole, the whole being Mary's peanuts. It's very easy to get confused doing it that way, because the numbers aren't concrete and they quickly become meaningless. The advantage of Plugging In is that you're working with actual amounts, just like real life. One more thing: We picked 15 because we expected it to work with the fractions in the problem. If we'd picked a number that didn't work well, we would have tried another number.

PLUGGING IN THE ANSWER CHOICES

Good news. Unlike the math tests you usually have in school, the SAT is primarily multiple choice. That means that on many problems, you don't have to generate your own answer to a problem. Instead, the answer will be one of the five answers sitting on the page right in front of you. All you have to figure out is *which* one of the five is the answer.

HOW TO RECOGNIZE QUESTIONS FOR PLUGGING IN THE ANSWER CHOICES

- The question will be straightforward—something like "How old is Bob?" or "How many potatoes are in the bag?" or "What was the original cost of the stereo?"

- The answer choices will be actual values.

HOW TO PLUG IN THE ANSWER CHOICES

Don't write an equation. Instead, pick an answer and work it through the steps of the problem, one at a time, and see if it works. In essence, you're asking *what if (C) is the answer? Does that solve the problem?*

Here's an example:

If $\dfrac{3(x-1)}{2} = \dfrac{9}{x-2}$, what is the value of x ?

(A) -4
(B) -2
(C) 1
(D) 4
(E) 9

Solution: Try (C) first. (You'll soon find out why.) Plug in 1 for x and see if the equation works:

$$\frac{3(1-1)}{2} = \frac{9}{1-2}$$

$$\frac{0}{2} = \frac{9}{-1}$$

Okay, so (C) isn't the answer. Cross it out. Try (D):

$$\frac{3(4-1)}{2} = \frac{9}{4-2}$$

$$\frac{9}{2} = \frac{9}{2}$$

The equation works, so (D) is the answer. Sure, you could have done the algebra, but wasn't plugging in easier? Once again, you've seen an algebra problem turned into an arithmetic problem, and all it required was managing simple operations like $4 - 1$. You're much more likely to make mistakes dealing with x than with $4 - 1$. Also, when you plug in, you're taking advantage of the fact that there are only five answer choices. One of them is correct. You might as well try them and find out which one it is—and you no longer have to face the horror of working out a problem algebraically and finding that your answer isn't one of the choices.

Here's a harder example:

> Paul had twice as many potatoes as Dan, who
> had the same number of potatoes as Zed. If
> Paul were to give five potatoes to Zed, then
> Dan would have three times as many potatoes
> as Paul. How many potatoes did Dan have?
>
> (A) 10
> (B)   6
> (C)   3
> (D)   2
> (E)   1

Solution: Try (C) first. If Dan started with 3, then Zed also started with 3. Since Paul had twice as many potatoes as Dan, then Paul started with 6. If he gives 5 to Zed, Paul now has 1 and Zed has 8. Dan still has 3 potatoes, which is three times as many as Paul. So (C) is the right answer. If (C) didn't work, you could keep trying until you found the answer that did.

To keep things organized, make a chart:

	D	Z	P
Originally:	3	3	6
After exchange:	3	8	1

TIPS FOR HAPPINESS WHEN PLUGGING IN THE ANSWER CHOICES

- (C) is a good answer to try first, unless it's awkward to work with.

- The answers will be in numerical order, so you will often be able to eliminate answers that are either too big or too small, based on the result you got with (C). If the answer to (C) was too small, you should try bigger answer choices. If the answer to (C) was too big, try smaller answer choices.

- Don't try to work out all the steps in advance—the nice thing about plugging in is that you do the steps one at a time.

- Plugging In questions may be long word problems or short arithmetic problems, and they can appear in the easy, medium, or difficult sections. The harder the question, the better off you'll be plugging in.

- Make a chart if you have a lot of stuff to keep track of.

QUICK QUIZ #2

EASY

6. If 4 less than the product of b and 6 is 44, what
    is the value of b ?

    (A) 2
    (B) 4
    (C) 6
    (D) 8
    (E) 14

MEDIUM

13. A store reduces the price of a CD player by 20%
    and then reduces that price by 15%. If the final
    price of the CD player is $170, what was its
    original price?

    (A) $140
    (B) $185
    (C) $200
    (D) $250
    (E) $275

HARD

20. Triangle ABC has sides measuring 2, 3, and r.
    Which of the following is a possible value for r ?

    (A) 0.5
    (B) 1
    (C) 2
    (D) 5
    (E) 6

Answers and Explanations: Quick Quiz #2

6. **D** Try (C) first, so $b = 6$. The product of 6 and 6 is 36, and 4 less than 36 is 32. 32 isn't 44, so cross out (C). Try a higher number, (D). If $b = 8$, the product of 8 and 6 is 48, and 4 less than 48 is 44.

13. **D** Try (C) first. If the original price of the CD player was $200, then 20% of 200 is 40. That leaves us with a price of $160. Hey—the final price was $170, and you're already below that. You need a higher number. Try (D): If the original price was $250, take 20% of 250 = 50. Now the price is $200. Take another 15% ($30) off and you get 200 − 30 = 170.

20. **C** You need to know a rule here—the sum of any 2 sides of a triangle must equal more than the third side. Try (C) first. If $r = 2$, then the sides are 2, 2, 3. Add up any pair and you get a number that's higher than the remaining number. So it works. (Try some of the other answers, just for practice, and see how they *don't* work.)

Do a little analysis. See how the questions got harder as you went along? In the easy question, you had to read carefully, multiply, and subtract. In the medium question, you had to take percentages. In the hard question, you had to deal with geometry without a diagram and also know a particular rule. For all the questions, plugging in allowed you to avoid writing an equation. Less work is good.

ESTIMATING

A Rough Estimate May Be All That's Necessary

The less work the better. Maybe you'll only be able to eliminate a couple of answers. That's okay too.

For example:

When .20202 is multiplied by 10^5 and then subtracted from 66,666, the result is

(A) −46,464
(B) 464.98
(C) 4,646.4
(D) 6,464.6
(E) 46,464

Solution: First multiply .20202 by 10^5. Just move the decimal point 5 places to the right. You get 20,202. (Use your calculator if you want.) Now you're going to subtract that from 66,666—but estimate it before you continue. Looks to be around 40,000 or so, doesn't it? So pick (E) and go on.

There are two advantages to solving the problem this way. First, you avoid having to do the last step of the problem and gain yourself some time. Second, you avoid even the possibility of making a careless mistake in that last step.

We know you can subtract. That's not the issue. On a timed test, with a lot of pressure on you, the fewer steps you have to do, the better off you are.

This is a fabulous piece of news—it means that you should use your eyes to estimate distances and angles, instead of jumping immediately to formulas and equations. You aren't allowed to bring a ruler or a protractor into the test. But you can often tell if one line is longer than another, or if the shaded part of a circle is larger than the unshaded part, just by estimating. That should allow you to eliminate at least a couple of answers, maybe more.

Is this a sketchy technique? Are we telling you to take the easy way out? No and yes. ETS, the company that writes the SAT, doesn't mind if you use your common sense. Neither do we. And as for the easy way out…yes, that's exactly what you're training yourself to look for.

Estimating is not totally foreign to you. Think of geometry problems you encounter in real life—parking a car, packing a box, even shooting a basketball. We guess you don't take out a pad and pencil and start calculating to solve any of these problems. You estimate them, and see what happens.

Same deal on the SAT.

For example:

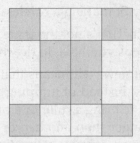

What fractional part of the square is shaded?

(A) $\frac{1}{4}$

(B) $\frac{3}{10}$

(C) $\frac{1}{2}$

(D) $\frac{7}{12}$

(E) $\frac{15}{16}$

Solution: Just look at it. How much looks shaded? A little? No, so cross out (A) and (B). Most of it? No, so cross out (E). That leaves you with two answer choices, which isn't bad, since you haven't done any math. If you get stuck here, guess. Or count up how many shaded squares there are, and put that over the total number of squares. So the fractional part is $\frac{8}{16}$, or $\frac{1}{2}$.

The answer is (C).

QUICK QUIZ #3

EASY

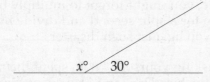

$x°$ $30°$

4. Which of the following is equal to $3x$?

   (A) 50
   (B) 120
   (C) 150
   (D) 360
   (E) 450

MEDIUM

13. Dan, Laura, and Jane went grocery shopping.
    Dan spent three times as much as Laura and
    half as much as Jane. If they spent a total of $50
    on groceries, how much did Jane spend?

    (A) $15
    (B) $20
    (C) $25
    (D) $30
    (E) $45

HARD

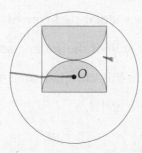

17. In the circle above with center O, the radius
    of the circle is equal to the length of a side of
    the square. If the shaded region represents two
    semicircles inscribed in the square, the ratio of
    the area of the shaded region to the area of the
    circle is

    (A) 1:16
    (B) 1:8
    (C) 1:4
    (D) 1:2
    (E) 2:3

ANSWERS AND EXPLANATIONS: QUICK QUIZ #3

4. **E** Angle x is pretty big, isn't it? So $3x$ is really, really big. Cross out (A), (B), and (C). Now work it out. $x + 30 = 180$, so $x = 150$. And $3x = 450$. If you fail to estimate, you might forget to multiply by 3 and pick (C). You might fall asleep for a split second and divide by 3 and pick (A). Estimating protects you against such disasters.

13. **D** You might start by asking yourself, "Who spent the most money?" Since Jane spent twice as much as Dan, and Dan spent three times as much as Laura, Jane spent the most. You can definitely eliminate (A); it's too small an amount for Jane to have spent. Now Plug In the answer choices. Begin with (C) or (D), since (A) is out. Which is the easier number to cut in half?

	J	D	L
(D)	30	15	5

    $30 + $15 + $5 = $50, so (D) is your answer.

17. **C** Look at the figure. How much of it looks shaded? Less than half? Sure. Cross out (D) and (E). If you're good at estimating, maybe you can cross out (A) as well. (Try drawing more semi-circles in the big circle and see how many will fit.) Now let's figure it out, using our good friend plugging in: Let the radius = 2. So the area is 4π. If the radius = 2, the side of the square is 2. The shaded part consists of 2 semi-circles, each with a radius that's $\frac{1}{2}$ the side of the square, so the radius of the small circle is 1, and the area is π. Put the small area over the big area and you get $\frac{\pi}{4\pi} = \frac{1}{4}$, which is a ratio of 1:4.

Tips for Estimating Happiness

- With geometry, especially on hard questions, the answer choices need to be translated into numbers that you can work with.

- Translate π to a bit more than 3; $\sqrt{2}$ is 1.4; $\sqrt{3}$ is 1.7.

- Practice estimating *a lot*, even if you're going to work out the problem—and notice how your estimates improve.

- The farther apart the answer choices, the bigger the opportunity for eliminating answers by estimating.

- If the figure is NOT drawn to scale, redraw it if you can, using whatever measurements are provided. Then go ahead and estimate. If you can't redraw it, don't estimate.

- If two things look about equal, you can't assume that they're *exactly* equal.

- Trust what your eyes tell you.

How to Apply These Techniques

To study efficiently for the SAT, you must:

- Practice plugging in. Plug in whenever and wherever you can.

- Analyze your work so that you can avoid making the same mistakes over and over.

- Do the problems in this book as though you are taking the real thing—practice with the same focus and intensity you will need on the actual SAT.

2
Arithmetic

Much of this chapter will be review, but study it well. Even though the SAT tests very basic mathematical concepts, these concepts are tested in very particular ways. To do well on the SAT requires that you know these definitions backward and forward.

After each section of review is a Quick Quiz with a variety of questions: easy, medium, and hard. If you get all of them right, you're in very good shape. And keep in mind: You could leave *all* the hard questions blank and still get a good score. So make sure you're getting the easy and medium ones right first.

DEFINITIONS

consecutive	numbers in order (1, 2, 3, etc.)
denominator	the bottom number of a fraction
difference	what you get when you subtract one number from another
digit	a number from 0 to 9. For example, 376 is a three-digit number.
distinct	different (i.e., the distinct factors of 4 are 1, 4, and 2—not 1, 4, 2, and 2)
even	a number evenly divisible by 2 (0 is even)
factor	same meaning as "division": a smaller number that goes into your number (example: 2 is a factor of 8)
multiple	a bigger number that your number goes into (example: 8 is a multiple of 2)
numerator	the top number of a fraction
odd	a number not evenly divisible by 2
PEMDAS	you won't see that written on the test—it's a handy acronym for the order of operations: Parentheses, Exponents, Multiplication, Division, Addition, Subtraction. Learn it, live it.
places	in 234.167, 2 is the hundreds place, 3 is the tens place, 4 is the ones or units digit, 1 is the tenths place, 6 is the hundredths place, and 7 is the thousandths place.
prime	a number divisible evenly only by itself and 1. The first five primes are 2, 3, 5, 7, and 11. (Note: 1 is *not* prime.)
product	what you get when you multiply two numbers together
quotient	what you get after dividing one number into another
reciprocal	whatever you multiply a number by to get 1 (i.e., the reciprocal of $\frac{1}{2}$ is $\frac{2}{1}$. The reciprocal of 6 is $\frac{1}{6}$.)
remainder	what's left over if a division problem doesn't work out evenly
sum	what you get when you add together two numbers

QUICK QUIZ #1

EASY

1. What is the greatest common prime factor of 32 and 28 ?

   (A) 1
   (B) 2
   (C) 3
   (D) 4
   (E) 7

A

MEDIUM

9. If x is a positive integer greater than 1, and $x(x + 4)$ is odd, then x must be

   (A) even
   (B) odd
   (C) prime
   (D) a factor of 8
   (E) divisible by 8

B

HARD

20. Each of prime numbers p and q is greater than 12, their difference is two, and there is no prime number between p and q. Which of the following is the least possible value of $p + q$?

    (A) 18
    (B) 24
    (C) 28
    (D) 36
    (E) 42

13   17   19

A

Answers and Explanations: Quick Quiz #1

1. **B** Plug in the answer choices. Why bother thinking up the answer yourself when they give you five choices? Since the question asks for the greatest common *prime* factor, you can cross out anything that isn't prime—get rid of (A) and (D). Now start with (E), because it's the greatest answer choice. Does 7 go into 32? No. Cross out (E). (C): Does 3 go into 28? No, cross out (C). That leaves us with (B). Does 2 go into 32 and 28? Yep.

9. **B** Plug in your own number for x. If x has to be a positive integer greater than 1, try $x = 2$. But $2(2 + 4)$ isn't odd. So try $x = 3$. $3(3 + 4) = 21$, which works. Now you can cross out everything but (B) and (C). Try an odd number that isn't prime, say $x = 9$. $9(9 + 4) = 117$, which is odd. So cross off (C).

20. **B** This question requires careful reading and a bit of trial by error. Both p and q must be greater than 12 and prime. The first prime numbers greater than 12 are 13 and 17, but they do not differ by two. The next two prime numbers are 17 and 19; these work. Their sum is 36.

DIVISIBILITY

On the SAT, **divisible** means divisible *evenly*, with no remainder. This means that 16 is divisible by 4, but 18 is *not* divisible by 4. To figure out whether one number is divisible by another, use your calculator.

Factoring shows up on the SAT all over the place. That's okay, it's easy.

To find all of the factors of a number, factor in pairs. Start with 1 and make a list of all the pairs that multiply together to equal the original number:

What are the factors of 36?

   1, 36
   2, 18
   3, 12
   4, 9
   6, 6

To find the **prime factors** of a number, simply find all the factors as shown above, and then select only those that are also prime numbers.

QUICK QUIZ #2

EASY

2. Which of the following could be a factor of $n(n + 1)$, if n is a positive integer less than 3 ?

   (A) 3
   (B) 4
   (C) 5
   (D) 8
   (E) 9

MEDIUM

10. If Darlene divided 210 chocolate kisses into bags containing the same number of kisses, each of the following could be the number of kisses per bag EXCEPT

    (A) 35
    (B) 21
    (C) 20
    (D) 15
    (E) 14

ANSWERS AND EXPLANATIONS: QUICK QUIZ #2

2. **A** Plug in. If $n = 1$, $1(1 + 1) = 2$. None of the answers are factors of 2. If $n = 2$, $2(2+1) = 6$. 3 is a factor of 6, so the answer is (A).

10. **C** You could use your calculator and divide each answer into 210, then pick the one that doesn't go evenly. Or you could factor 210 as $7 \times 5 \times 3 \times 2$. Now factor the answers. (A): 7×5, which goes in, so cross it out. (B): 7×3. Cross it out. (C): $2 \times 2 \times 5$. That doesn't go in because there's only one factor of 2 in 210.

FRACTIONS

To add fractions, get a common denominator and then add across the top:

$$\frac{1}{2} + \frac{2}{3} = \frac{3}{6} + \frac{4}{6} = \frac{7}{6}$$

To subtract fractions, it's the same deal, but subtract across the top:

$$\frac{3}{4} - \frac{1}{3} = \frac{9}{12} - \frac{4}{12} = \frac{5}{12}$$

To multiply fractions, cancel if you can, then multiply across, top and bottom:

$$\frac{1}{2} \cdot \frac{3}{5} = \frac{3}{10} \qquad\qquad \frac{2}{7} \cdot \frac{\overset{2}{\cancel{14}}}{9} = \frac{4}{19}$$
$$\phantom{\frac{2}{7} \cdot} {}_{1}$$

To divide fractions, flip the second one, then multiply across, top and bottom:

$$\frac{2}{3} \div \frac{1}{2} = \frac{2}{3} \cdot \frac{2}{1} = \frac{4}{3}$$

To see which of the two fractions is bigger, cross-multiply from bottom to top. The side with the bigger product is the bigger fraction.

$$55 \diagdown \frac{5}{7} \diagup \diagdown \frac{8}{11} \diagup 56$$

56 is bigger than 55, so $\frac{8}{11}$ is bigger.

QUICK QUIZ #3

EASY

3. Which of the following is greatest?

   (A) $\dfrac{3}{5} \times \dfrac{5}{3} =$

   (B) $\dfrac{3}{5} \div \dfrac{5}{3} =$

   (C) $\dfrac{3}{5} + \dfrac{3}{5} =$

   (D) $\dfrac{5}{3} - \dfrac{3}{5} =$

   (E) $\dfrac{5}{3} \div \dfrac{3}{5} =$

MEDIUM

13. In a jar of cookies, there is $\dfrac{1}{6}$ probability of randomly selecting an oatmeal-raisin cookie and a $\dfrac{1}{8}$ probability of selecting a sugar cookie. If the remaining cookies are all chocolate chip cookies, then which one of the following could be the number of cookies in the jar?

    (A) 14
    (B) 16
    (C) 20
    (D) 24
    (E) 32

HARD

20. At a track meet, $\frac{2}{5}$ of the first-place finishers attended Southport High School, and $\frac{1}{2}$ of them were girls. If $\frac{2}{9}$ of the first-place finishers who did NOT attend Southport High School were girls, what fractional part of the total number of first-place finishers were boys?

(A) $\frac{1}{9}$

(B) $\frac{2}{15}$

(C) $\frac{7}{18}$

(D) $\frac{3}{5}$

(E) $\frac{2}{3}$

ANSWERS AND EXPLANATIONS: QUICK QUIZ #3

3. **E** You can do some estimating here, but be careful—remember that when you divide by a fraction, you're really multiplying by the reciprocal. (E) is $\frac{5}{3} \div \frac{3}{5}$, which is $\frac{5}{3} \times \frac{5}{3} = \frac{25}{9}$. (A): 1. (B): $\frac{9}{25}$. (C): $\frac{6}{5}$. (D): $\frac{16}{25}$. If you had trouble figuring out any of those, go back to the fraction review.

13. **D** Plug in the answers. Start with (C). If there are 20 cookies in the jar, how many oatmeal-raisin cookies are there? Not a whole number, so this can't be correct. While it is not clear whether you need a bigger or smaller number, you now see that you need a number that is divisible by both six and eight, so both fractions will yield a whole number. Only (D) works.

20. **E** Plug in. The total number of first-place finishers was 30. You can find the number who were from Southport by taking $\frac{2}{5}$ of 30 = 12. That leaves 18 who did not go to Southport High School. If half the 12 Southport runners were girls, that means 6 were girls and 6 were boys. If $\frac{2}{9}$ of the non-Southport runners were girls, then $\frac{2}{9}$ of 18 = 4 girls, which leaves 14 boys. That means a total of 14 + 6 = 20 boys, out of a total of 30, or $\frac{20}{30} = \frac{2}{3}$. You will be happier if you make a tree chart:

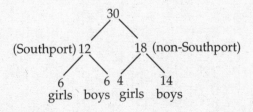

DECIMALS

To add, subtract, multiply, or divide decimals, use your calculator. Remember to check each number as you punch it in, and be extra careful with the decimal point.

To convert a fraction to a decimal, use your calculator to divide the numerator by the denominator:

$$\frac{1}{2} = 1 \div 2 = .5 \qquad \frac{5}{8} = 5 \div 8 = .625 \qquad \frac{4}{3} = 1.333$$

To convert a decimal to a fraction, count up the number of digits to the right of the decimal point and put that many zeros in your denominator:

$$0.2 = \frac{2}{10} \qquad .314 = \frac{314}{1000} \qquad 2.23 = \frac{223}{100}$$

QUICK QUIZ #4

EASY

1. If $0.2p = 4$, then $4p =$

   (A) 0.2
   (B) 2
   (C) 8
   (D) 40
   (E) 80

MEDIUM

10. For positive integers y and z, if $z^2 = y^3$ and $y^2 = 16$, then $\dfrac{y}{z} =$

    (A) 0.8
    (B) 0.5
    (C) 0.4
    (D) 0.2
    (E) 2

HARD

19. $\dfrac{\dfrac{ad}{bc}}{\dfrac{ac}{bd}} =$

    (A) 1

    (B) a^2c^2

    (C) $\dfrac{a^2}{b^2}$

    (D) $\dfrac{d^2}{c^2}$

    (E) b^2d^2

ANSWERS AND EXPLANATIONS: QUICK QUIZ #4

1. **E** If $0.2p = 4$, then $p = 20$, and $4p = 80$.

10. **B** If $y^2 = 16$, then $y = 4$. If $z^2 = y^3$, then $z^2 = 64$ and $z = 8$.

So $\dfrac{y}{z} = \dfrac{4}{8} = \dfrac{1}{2} = 0.5$.

19. **D** Remember that to divide fractions you flip the denominator and multiply. (Dividing is the same as multiplying by the reciprocal.)

So $\dfrac{\frac{ad}{bc}}{\frac{ac}{bd}} = \dfrac{ad}{bc} \bullet \dfrac{bd}{ac} = \dfrac{adbd^2}{abc^2} = \dfrac{d^2}{c^2}$.

PERCENTAGES

For some reason, many people get hung up on percents, probably because they are trying to remember a series of operations rather than using their common sense.

A percentage is simply a fractional part—50% of something is one-half of something, and 47% is a little less than half. It is very helpful to approximate percents in this way, and not to think of them as abstract, meaningless numbers. 3.34% is very little of something, 0.0012% a tiny part of something, and 105% a little more than the whole.

Keep in mind that since percents are an expression of the fractional part, they do not represent actual numbers. If, for example, you're a salesperson, and you earn a 15% commission on what you sell, you'll get a lot richer selling Rolls-Royces than you will selling doughnuts. Even thousands of doughnuts. All examples of 15% are not created equal, unless they are 15% of the same number.

Now for the nitty-gritty:

To convert a percent to a decimal, move the decimal point two spaces to the left:

$$50\% = .5 \qquad 4\% = .04 \qquad .03\% = .0003 \qquad 112\% = 1.12$$

To convert a decimal to a percent, move the decimal point two spaces to the right:

$$.5 = 50\% \qquad .66 = 66\% \qquad .01 = 1\% \qquad 4 = 400\%$$

To convert a percent to a fraction, put the number over 100:

$$50\% = \frac{50}{100} \qquad 4\% = \frac{4}{100} \qquad 106\% = \frac{106}{100} \qquad x = \frac{x}{100}$$

To get a percent of a number, multiply by the decimal. So to get 22% of 50, first change the percentage to a decimal by moving the decimal point two places to the left = .22. Then multiply on your calculator.

The second way to get a percent of a number is to translate your sentence into an equation. This is easier than it sounds. Convert the percent to a fraction and substitute × for *of*, = for *is*, and *x* for *what*.

What is 50% of 16?

This question translates to $x = \dfrac{50}{100} \times 16$.

This method is particularly useful for complicated percents:

What is 10% of 40% of 22?

This question translates to $x = \dfrac{10}{100} \times \dfrac{40}{100} \times 22$.

To calculate what percent one number is of another number, use the translation method, substituting $\dfrac{x}{100}$ for *what percent*.

What percent of 16 is 8?

This question translates to $\dfrac{x}{100} \times 16 = 8$.

8 is what percent of 16?

This question translates to $8 = \dfrac{x}{100} \times 16$.

Notice that even though these equations look a little different, they will produce the same answer.

QUICK QUIZ #5

EASY

3. If 20% of p is 10, then 10% of p is

   (A) 2
   (B) 4
   (C) 5
   (D) 8
   (E) 14

MEDIUM

11. Mabel agreed to pay the tax and tip for dinner at a restaurant with her four friends. Each of the friends paid an equal part of the cost of the dinner, which was $96. If the tax and tip together were 20% of the cost of the meal, Mabel paid how much less than any one of her friends?

    (A) $2.40
    (B) $4.80
    (C) $9.20
    (D) $19.20
    (E) $24.00

HARD

18. If 200% of 40% of x is equal to 40% of y, then x is what percent of y ?

    (A) 10%
    (B) 20%
    (C) 30%
    (D) 50%
    (E) 80%

3. **C** 10% is half of 20%, and half of 10 is 5. That way you don't have to worry about p. To figure p, translate the sentence: $\frac{20}{100} \times p = 10$.

$\frac{p}{5} = 10$, and $p = 50$. Now do the next step: $0.1 \times 50 = 5$.

11. **B** First calculate what each friend paid: $96 \div 4 = \$24$. Now do the percentage: $0.20 \times 96 = \$19.20$. Subtract the second number from the first. If you noticed that each of the four friends paid 25%, and Mabel paid 20%, you could take a fast shortcut by taking the difference, or 5% of 96. [If you picked (D) or (E), you should reread the question before picking your final answer.]

18. **D** Plug in $100 = x$. 40% of 100 is 40, and 200% of 40 is $2 \times 40 = 80$. Now our question says that 80 is 40% of y, so $y = 200$, and $(80 = 0.4y)$. The question asks "x is what percent of y?", which you can write out as $100 = \frac{p}{100} \times 200$. Or you can simply realize that 100 is half of 200, which is 50%.

MORE ON PERCENTAGES

To calculate percent increase or decrease, use the following formula:

$$\text{percent increase or decrease} = \frac{\text{difference}}{\text{original amount}} \times 100$$

For instance, if a \$40 book was reduced to \$35, the difference in price is \$5. Therefore, the percent decrease is equal to $\frac{5}{40} \times 100$, which is the same as $\frac{1}{8} \times 100$ or 12.5%.

QUICK QUIZ #6

MEDIUM

14. A store owner buys a pound of grapes for 80 cents and sells it for a dollar. What percent of the selling price of grapes is the store owner's profit?

    (A) 10%
    (B) 20%
    (C) 25%
    (D) 40%
    (E) 80%

HARD

17. On the first test of the semester, Barbara scored a 60. On the last test of the semester, Barbara scored a 75. By what percent did Barbara's score improve?

    (A) 12%
    (B) 15%
    (C) 18%
    (D) 20%
    (E) 25%

14. **B** First determine the store owner's profit. Change everything to cents so that you're only working with one unit: $100 - 80 = 20$. Now translate the question into math terms: $\frac{x}{100} \bullet 100 = 20$.

17. **E** Find the difference: $75 - 60 = 15$. Put this difference (15) over the lower number: $\frac{15}{60}$. Reduce the fraction to $\frac{1}{4}$, which is 25%. Or divide it on your calculator, which will give you 0.25. Convert it to a percentage by moving the decimal two places to the right.

> Estimating is always a good idea when you're doing a percentage question—a lot of the time there are silly answers that you can cross out before you do any math at all.

RATIOS

A ratio is like a percentage—it tells you how much you have of one thing compared to how much you have of another thing. For example, if you have hats and T-shirts in a ratio of 2:3, then for every two hats, you have three T-shirts. What we don't know is the actual number of each. It could be two hats and three T-shirts. Or it could be four hats and six T-shirts. Or 20 hats and 30 T-shirts.

A ratio describes a relationship, not a total number.

Whenever you need to convert from a ratio in its most reduced form to real-life numbers, there are two key steps:

- Always add the ratio numbers to get a whole.

- Find the factor that connects a ratio number to its real-life counterpart. All of the ratio numbers get multiplied by this factor to convert to real-life numbers.

A great way to see those two steps in action is to use a Ratio Box.

2. In Mr. Peterson's class of 48 students, the ratio of boys to girls is 3:5.

Boys	Girls	Whole
3 +	5 =	8	← Ratio
×	×	×	← Multiply by
=	=	6
=	=	=
+	=	48	← Actual number

i.   How many girls are in the class? _____
ii. How many boys are in the class? _____
iii. Boys make up what fractional part of the class? _____
iv. If you answered $\frac{18}{48}$ above, what does that reduce to? _____

Don't get the order of the ratio mixed up—if the problem says red marbles and blue marbles in a ratio of 1:2, the first number represents the red marbles and the second number represents the blue marbles.

QUICK QUIZ #7

MEDIUM

12. If $\dfrac{x}{y} = \dfrac{4}{3}$ and $\dfrac{x}{k} = \dfrac{1}{2}$, then $\dfrac{k}{y} =$

   (A) $\dfrac{1}{6}$

   (B) $\dfrac{3}{8}$

   (C) $\dfrac{2}{3}$

   (D) $\dfrac{3}{2}$

   (E) $\dfrac{8}{3}$

16. The junior class at Mooreland High is composed of boys and girls in a ratio of 5:1. All of the following could be the number of students in the junior class EXCEPT

   (A) 12
   (B) 24
   (C) 42
   (D) 54
   (E) 62

HARD

20. In a certain ocean region, the ratio of sharks to tuna to damselfish to guppies is 1 to 3 to 5 to 6. If there are 1,500 total fish in that region, how many of the fish are sharks?

   (A) 15
   (B) 100
   (C) 150
   (D) 300
   (E) 450

12. **E** Since $x = 4$ in one ratio and $x = 1$ in the other, you can't compare them. First make them equal. If you multiply the second ratio by $\frac{4}{4}$, you get $\frac{4}{4}$. (Notice that if you multiply all parts of the ratio by the same number, it doesn't change. It just takes an unreduced form.) Now the x's are the same in both ratios, so you can compare them, and $\frac{k}{y} = \frac{8}{3}$. You could also plug in, which would work at least as well.

16. **E** If the ratio is 5:1, you can add the parts and get 6 students. Therefore, the number of students in the class must be a multiple of 6. All of the choices are multiples of 6 except (E).

20. **B** Make the ratio box. There are always three rows: ratio, multiply by, and actual. Here, the columns are: sharks, tuna, damselfish, guppies, and Total. In the first row, enter the ratio numbers: 1, 3, 5, and 6. Add them up, and put the sum (15) under Total. As the actual total is 1,500, enter that number in the lower, right cell. What times 15 is 1,500? 100. So, enter 100 in all of the multiply by cells. You can solve for all four fish types by multiplying the ratio number by 100, or just solve for sharks, as that is the question.

PROPORTIONS

To set up a proportion, match categories on top and bottom. For example:

> If 10 nails cost 4 cents, how much do 50 nails cost?

$$\text{(nails)} \quad \frac{10}{4} = \frac{50}{x} \quad \text{(cents)}$$

$$10x = 200, \text{ so } x = 20 \text{ cents}$$

The great thing about proportions is that it doesn't matter which is on top—if you match nails to nails and cents to cents (or whatever), you'll get the right answer. Be consistent.

To solve an **inverse variation** problem, use the following set-up.

$$x_1 y_1 = x_2 y_2$$

If the value of x is inversely proportional to the value of y and $y = 4$ when $x = 15$, what is the value of x when y is 12?

$$x(12) = (15)(4)$$
$$x = 5$$

To solve rate problems, set up a proportion:

If Bonzo rode his unicycle 30 miles in 5 hours, how long would it take him to ride 12 miles at the same rate?

$$\text{(miles)} \quad \frac{30}{5} = \frac{12}{x} \quad \text{(hours)}$$

$$30x = 60$$

$$x = 2 \text{ hours}$$

QUICK QUIZ #8

EASY

2. Laura can solve 6 math questions in 12 minutes. Working at the same rate, how many minutes would it take Laura to solve 5 math questions?

    (A) 6
    (B) 8
    (C) 9
    (D) 10
    (E) 11

MEDIUM

8. The length of time in hours that a certain battery will last is inversely proportional to the length of time in years that the battery spends in storage. If the battery spends 3 years in storage, it will last 25 hours, so how long must the battery have been in storage if it will last 15 hours?

    (A) 1.75 years

    (B) 5 years

    (C) 7.5 years

    (D) $41\frac{2}{3}$ years

    (E) 75 years

HARD

16. A factory produced 15 trucks of the same model. If the trucks had a combined weight of $34\frac{1}{2}$ tons, how much, in pounds, did one of the trucks weigh? (One ton = 2000 pounds)

    (A)   460
    (B) 2200
    (C) 4500
    (D) 4600
    (E) 5400

2. **D** $\frac{6}{12} = \frac{5}{x}$. Cross-multiply to get $6x = 60$ and $x = 10$.

8. **B** To do this problem, it is important to know the formula for inverse variation: $x_1 y_1 = x_2 y_2$. In this case, the x_1 is 3 years, y_1 is 25 hours, and y_2 is 15 hours. So set up the equation as follows: $3 \times 25 = x_2 \times 15$. $\frac{75}{15} = x_2 = 5$ years.

16. **D** You can do this two ways: You can convert from tons to pounds first or do it later. If you do it first, multiply 34.5×2000. That gives you 69,000. Your proportion should look like this: $\frac{15}{69,000} = \frac{1}{x}$. So $15x = 69,000$, and $x = 4600$. Or you can divide 15 into 34.5, which gives you 2.3 tons per truck. Then multiply 2.3 times 2000.

AVERAGES

You already know how to figure out an average. You can figure out your GPA, right?

To get the average (arithmetic mean) of a set of numbers, add them up, then divide by the number of things in the set:

What's the average of 3, 5, and 10? $3 + 5 + 10 = 18$ and $18 \div 3 = 6$.

Most of the time on the SAT you are not given a set of numbers and asked for the average—they want to make their questions a little harder than that. There are three elements at work here: the sum of the numbers, the number of things in the set, and the average. To get any of these elements, you need to know the other two.

The easy way to remember these relationships is by memorizing the "Average Pie."

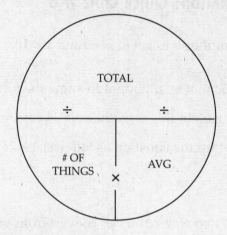

If you want to find any one element, cover it up, and what remains is the formula for finding it.

- The sum divided by the number of things = the average.

- The sum divided by the average = the number of things.

- The average multiplied by the number of things = the sum.

To solve an average problem, put whatever elements you are given into the average pie, and solve for the remaining element. The problem will always give you two parts out of the three, which will enable you to solve for the third.

QUICK QUIZ #9

EASY

6. The average of 3 numbers is 22, and the smallest of these numbers is 2. If the other two numbers are equal, each of them is

    (A) 22
    (B) 30
    (C) 32
    (D) 40
    (E) 64

MEDIUM

12. Caroline scored 85, 88, and 89 on three of her four history tests. If her average score for all tests was 90, what did she score on her fourth test?

    (A) 89
    (B) 90
    (C) 93
    (D) 96
    (E) 98

HARD

14. The average of 8, 13, x, and y is 6. The average of 15, 9, x, and x is 8. What is the value of y ?

    (A) −1
    (B) 0
    (C) 4
    (D) 6
    (E) 8

Answers and Explanations: Quick Quiz #9

6. **C** If the average of 3 numbers is 22, then their sum is 3×22 or 66. Take away the 2 and you've got 64 left. If the other two numbers are equal, divide 64 by 2 = 32.

12. **E** Caroline's final average was 90 on 4 tests. Therefore you can use the average pie to figure out the total number of points she had on those four tests, by multiplying $90 \times 4 = 360$. You also know her scores on the first three tests, so if you subtract $360 - 85 - 88 - 89$, you get 98 points, which is the total score she must have gotten on her fourth test.

14. **A** Since the average of 8, 13, x, and y is 6, you know that their total must be equal to 6×4 or 24. This means that $8 + 13 + x + y = 24$. If you subtract the 8 and the 13, you find that $x + y = 3$. You also know that the average of 15, 9, x, and x is 8, so their total must be equal to 32. $15 + 9 + x + x = 32$, so $x + x$ must equal 8, and $x = 4$. Since you know from earlier that $x + y = 3$, $y = -1$.

MEDIAN, MODE, SET, INTERSECTION, UNION, AND RANGE

Each of these terms involves finding a value or values in **sets** of numbers. A **set** is just a fancy term for a list of numbers.

The most common type of set question involves median.

To find the median, first put the group of numbers in ascending order. If the group has an odd number of elements, the median is the middle number.

> set: 1, 4, 9, 18, 54   median: 9
> set: 2, 4, 4, 4, 5   median: 4

If the group has an even number of elements, the median is *the average (arithmetic mean) of* the two middle numbers.

> set: 3, 15, 17, 74   median: 16
> set: 1, 6, 7, 8   median: 6.5

The remaining types of set questions are quite rare:

To find the mode, just look to see which number in the group appears the most often.

> set: 1, 1, 3, 5, 3, 4, 22, 3, 6   mode: 3
> set: 2, 5, 9, 11, 11, 15, 22   mode: 11

To find the intersection, list all the elements common to both sets.

> set: 2, 5, 8, 9, 12, 17
> set: 5, 9, 17, 25, 43   intersection: 5, 9, 17

To find the union, list all of the elements in each set.

> set: 2, 11, 13, 19, 33, 41
> set: 4, 8, 18, 19, 39, 75   union: 2, 4, 8, 11, 13, 18, 19, 33, 39, 41, 75

Note that even though the number 19 appears in both sets, it is only listed once for purposes of finding the union.

To find the range, subtract the smallest number from the largest.

> set: 3, 15, 28, 33, 33, 33, 42   range: 39

QUICK QUIZ #10

EASY

Set Q: {10, 2, 3, 5, 1, 7, 5, 2}

6. If the smallest and largest numbers in Set Q are removed, what is the median of Set Q ?

   (A) 3.5
   (B) 4
   (C) 5
   (D) 6
   (E) 7

MEDIUM

High Temperatures

Temperature	Number of days
22	2
25	2
28	3
31	0
34	4
37	1
40	2

12. Janet recorded the number of days certain high temperatures were reached over a 14-day period. She later decided to add data for one more day. If the high temperature on that day was 37, what is the median temperature for the set of days?

    (A) 26.5
    (B) 28
    (C) 31
    (D) 34
    (E) 35.5

HARD

18. If a set of 9 randomly selected numbers is generated, which one of the following changes CANNOT affect the value of the median?

    (A) Subtracting 2 from each number
    (B) Taking the square of each number
    (C) Decreasing the largest number only
    (D) Decreasing the smallest number only
    (E) Increasing the largest and smallest numbers only

Answers and Explanations: Quick Quiz #10

6. **B** Take out 10 and 1. Now write down the numbers in order: 2, 2, 3, 5, 5, 7. The middle of the list falls between 3 and 5, so the median is 4.

12. **D** On a median question, it is essential to list out all of the numbers, including all of the repeated numbers. The original list of numbers, in order, is:

    22, 22, 25, 25, 28, 28, 28, 34, 34, 34, 34, 37, 40, 40

    Once the new number is added the set of numbers is:

    22, 22, 25, 25, 28, 28, 28, 34, 34, 34, 34, 37, 37, 40, 40

    The middle number of the new list is 34. If you picked (C), you chose the original median.

18. **D** Write out any set of nine numbers, such as 1 through 9. The median is 5. If you subtract 2 from each number, the median changes to 3, so (A) is wrong. If you square each number, the median changes to 25, so (B) is wrong. If you decrease the largest number to 4 or less, the median will change to 4, so (C) is wrong. On the other hand, no matter how much you decrease the smallest number, the median will remain the same, so (D) is correct. (E) is wrong because increasing the smallest number to 6 or more will change the median.

EXPONENTS AND ROOTS

An exponent tells you how many times to multiply a number by itself. So x^3 is really shorthand for $x \cdot x \cdot x$. If you have a momentary lapse and can't remember the following rules, it may help to write out your problem the long way and work from there.

For exponents with the same base, remember MADSPM:

To Multiply, Add the exponents: $x^2 \cdot x^5 = x^{2+5} = x^7$

To Divide, Subtract the exponents: $x^6 \div x^3 = x^{6-3} = x^3$

To raise the Power, Multiply: $(x^4)^3 = x^{4 \times 3} = x^{12}$

You cannot add or subtract different exponents, so $x^6 + x^3$ is just $x^6 + x^3$. You can't reduce it.

For exponents with different bases:

The trick is to try to rewrite the numbers in terms of the same base. For example:

$$6^2 \times 12^4$$
$$\text{becomes}$$
$$6^2 \times (6 \times 2)^4 = 6^2 \times 6^4 \times 2^4$$

Now you can combine terms with the same base as above.

To deal with exponents and parentheses, remember that the exponent carries over to all parts within the parentheses:

$$2(3a^3)^2 = 2[(3^2)(a^6)] = 2(9a^6) = 18a^6$$

Keep in mind that 1 raised to any power is still just 1. ($1^{357} = 1$.)

Negative numbers with even exponents are positive; negative numbers with odd exponents are negative. Fractions with exponents get smaller, not bigger.

A **square root** is just a backward exponent; in other words, the number under the $\sqrt{}$ is what you get when you raise a number to a power of 2.

$$\sqrt{4} = 2 \qquad\qquad \sqrt{36} = 6 \qquad\qquad \sqrt{1} = 1$$

To multiply or divide square roots, just multiply or divide as usual.

$$\sqrt{7} \bullet \sqrt{3} = \sqrt{21} \qquad\qquad \sqrt{15} \div \sqrt{3} = \sqrt{5}$$

To add or subtract square roots, first make sure you have the same number under the $\sqrt{}$. Then add or subtract the number outside of the $\sqrt{}$.

$$5\sqrt{3} + 2\sqrt{3} = 7\sqrt{3} \qquad 6\sqrt{2} - \sqrt{2} = 5\sqrt{2}$$

Note that:

- A square root multiplied by itself is just that number without the $\sqrt{}$. $\left(\sqrt{3} \bullet \sqrt{3} = 3\right)$

- The square root of a fraction gets bigger. For example, $\sqrt{\dfrac{1}{4}} = \dfrac{1}{2}$.

- The square root of a number is always positive (on the SAT, anyway).

- The square root of 1 is 1.

Rational exponents combine powers with roots. To simplify the following expression:

$$8^{\frac{2}{3}}$$

First we raise the base to the power of the numerator of the fraction. In this case, the numerator is two, so we'll square the base and get the following:

$$8^2 = 64$$

Now we'll deal with the denominator of the fraction. The denominator tells us what root to take the number to. In this case, the denominator is three, so we'll find the third root and end up with the following:

$$\sqrt[3]{64} = 4$$

QUICK QUIZ #12

EASY

1. If $(3x)^2 = 81$, then $x =$

   (A) 2
   (B) 3
   (C) 6
   (D) 9
   (E) 12

MEDIUM

16. If $a > 0$, $b < 1$, and $c < 0$, assuming $b \neq 0$, which of the following must be true?

    (A) abc is positive.

    (B) abc is negative.

    (C) $a^2 b^2 c$ is positive.

    (D) $ab^2 c^2$ is positive.

    (E) $a^3 b^3 c^3$ is negative.

HARD

18. Which one of the following must be greater than x, if x is a real number?

    (A) $\dfrac{x}{4}$

    (B) $4x$

    (C) $x^2 + 1$

    (D) $x^3 + 1$

    (E) $\sqrt{x}$

1. **B** Square everything within the parentheses, so you get $3^2x^2 = 81$, or $9x^2 = 81$. Divide by 9 and you get $x^2 = 9$, and x could equal 3.

16. **D** Your life will be easier if you make a little chart showing the signs of each variable:

    $a +$

    $b\ ?$

    $c -$

    Now go to the answers. If you don't know the sign of b, you don't know the sign of (A), (B), or (E). In (C), a^2 is positive, b^2 will have to be positive no matter what the sign of b is, and c is negative. So the whole thing is negative. The answer is (D).

18. **C** Because there are variables in the answer choices, plug in. Start with an easy number, such as $x = 2$. (A) is less than x, so eliminate it. (B) is greater than x, so keep it. (C) is greater than x, so keep it as well. So is (D). (E) is less than x, so eliminate it. Now try a different type of number. If you try 0 or a fraction, you'll get rid of (B), but not (C) or (D). Try a negative number, such as –3. While (C) is still greater than x, (D) is not.

PROBABILITY AND ARRANGEMENTS

Probability measures the likelihood something will happen:

$$\text{Probability} = \frac{\text{What You Want}}{\text{What You Have}}$$

Here's an example:

In a small garden of flowers, 3 are daisies, 4 are sunflowers, 2 are gardenias, and 3 are carnations. If a flower is selected at random, what is the probability that it will be a gardenia?

Solution: As there are 2 gardenias, the numerator of the fraction is 2. As there are 12 flowers in all, the denominator of the fraction is 12. Thus, the probability of selecting a gardenia is $\frac{2}{12}$ or $\frac{1}{6}$.

Questions about **arrangements** ask such questions as how many ways there are to order something or how many outfits are possible. These are easy to solve if you follow the steps shown for this example:

A restaurant offers a three-course dinner menu from which a person can select 1 of 4 appetizers, 1 of 5 main courses, and 1 of 3 desserts. How many different combinations of appetizer, main course, and dessert are possible?

As we are selecting three different items, first draw three slots as place-holders:

____ ____ ____

Let's use the first slot for appetizers. How many appetizers are there, any one of which might be selected? 4, so write 4 above the slot. The next slot is for main course. How many main courses are there, any one of which can be selected? 5, so write 5 above the slot. The final slot is for dessert. As there are 3 desserts from which the selection can be made, write 3 in that slot. Your slots now look like this:

4   5   3

The final step is to multiply. $4 \times 5 \times 3 = 60$. That's it!

QUICK QUIZ #14

EASY

5. What is the probability of randomly choosing a white marble from a bag that contains 4 white marbles, 2 blue marbles, and 3 green marbles?

   (A) $\frac{1}{4}$

   (B) $\frac{2}{5}$

   (C) $\frac{2}{7}$

   (D) $\frac{4}{9}$

   (E) $\frac{4}{5}$

MEDIUM

11. In a drawer of socks, the probability of selecting a black pair of socks is $\frac{3}{8}$, and there are $\frac{1}{3}$ as many blue pairs of socks as there are black pairs of socks. If there are 12 brown pairs of socks, how many socks are there in the drawer?

    (A) 16
    (B) 24
    (C) 32
    (D) 40
    (E) 48

HARD

18. Janice has 3 belts (one blue, one red, and one green), 3 bracelets (one blue, one red, and one green), and 3 scarves (one blue, one red, and one green). If Janice wants to create an outfit containing a belt, a bracelet, and a scarf such that each item is a different color, how many possible outfits can she create?

    (A) 6
    (B) 9
    (C) 15
    (D) 21
    (E) 27

Answers and Explanations: Quick Quiz #14

5. **D** The total number of marbles is 9, and 4 of them are white. That means there's a 4-in-9 chance of picking a white marble. Keep in mind that the total goes on the bottom and the part goes on the top, which gives you $\frac{4}{9}$. $\frac{9}{4}$ isn't one of the choices here, but a lot of people might have wanted to pick it. Be careful.

11. **B** You can plug in the answers. Start with (C). If $\frac{3}{8}$ of the pairs of socks are black, there are 12 pairs of black socks ($\frac{3}{8} \times 32$). As there are $\frac{1}{3}$ as many pairs of blue socks as pairs of black socks, there are 4 pairs of blue socks ($\frac{1}{3} \times 12$). Add the 12 pairs of brown socks to the pairs of black and blue socks to get 28 socks—not 32. At this point, it may not be clear whether to pick a bigger number or a smaller number, so just pick a direction. If the answer is even further off, then switch directions. Try a smaller number. If $\frac{3}{8}$ of the pairs of socks are black, there are 9 pairs of black socks ($\frac{3}{8} \times 24$). As there are $\frac{1}{3}$ as many pairs of blue socks as pairs of black socks, there are 3 pairs of blue socks ($\frac{1}{3} \times 9$). Add the 12 pairs of brown socks to the pairs of black and blue socks to get 24 socks—exactly what you wanted.

18. **A** Set up a slot for each of the three items. Start with the belt. How many belts are there, any one of which Janice might select? 3, so write 3 in the first slot. Move on to the bracelet. This time, there are only 2 bracelets she might choose, as she has already chosen a belt in a particular color—that color cannot be repeated. So, write 2 in the second slot. From the scarves, Janice may select only 1, as the other two colors are already chosen, so write 1 in the last slot. Multiply to get 6. If you picked (E), you did not account for the restriction on colors; there are 27 possible combinations, but only 6 involving all three colors.

SEQUENCES

Most **sequence** problems ask you to find a repeating pattern in a set of numbers.

To attack sequence problems, write out the pattern until it repeats itself. Then extend the pattern out until you can answer the question.

> A rainbow bracelet has a repeating sequence of beads that repeat in the following order: red, orange, yellow, green, blue, violet. What is the color of the 602nd bead?

First write out the pattern:

> Red, orange, yellow, green, blue, violet, red, orange, yellow, green, blue, violet

Notice that the pattern repeats itself after every six beads. That means that every multiple of six will be violet, the sixth bead in the pattern. What multiple of six is closest to 602? 600 is a good choice. Thus…

600	601	602
Violet	Red	Orange

The 602nd bead is orange.

QUICK QUIZ #15

EASY

4. A certain list contains 11 consecutive multiples of 3. The first number is 21. What is the middle number?

(A) 26
(B) 27
(C) 36
(D) 39
(E) 51

MEDIUM

11. The first three numbers of a sequence are 1, 3, and 5, respectively. Every number in the sequence beyond the first three numbers can be found by taking the three preceding numbers, subtracting the second from the first, and adding the third. Which of the following is the sum of the first 40 numbers of the above sequence?

(A) 6
(B) 12
(C) 24
(D) 120
(E) 480

ANSWERS AND EXPLANATIONS: QUICK QUIZ #15

4. **C** The middle number in the list is the sixth term. Don't write out all the terms; just list them up to the sixth one: 21, 24, 27, 30, 33, **36.**

11. **D** If you follow the sequence out, the next number is 3, and then if you keep following the instructions, the sequence repeats itself (1,3,5,3 1,3,5,3 1,3,5,3 1,3,5,3) in sets of 4. So, take the first four numbers and find the sum (12) and multiply by 10 since you actually want the first 40 numbers.

3
Algebra

In the section on strategy, we gave you some ways to avoid algebra altogether—but you still need to be able to work with simple equations and review some other algebraic principles that don't exactly crop up in everyday life.

SIMPLE EQUATIONS

Sometimes you can plug in with these, sometimes not. You will definitely need to be comfortable manipulating equations to do well on the SAT.

To solve a simple equation, get the variable on one side of the equals sign and the numbers on the other.

$$9x - 4 = 12 + x$$
$$8x - 4 = 12$$
$$8x = 16$$
$$x = 2$$

We just added 4 to both sides and subtracted x from both sides. Then we divided both sides by 8. You can add, subtract, multiply, or divide either side of an equation, but remember that what you do to one side you have to do to the other.

Polynomial equations look tricky but follow all the same rules of simple equations. You can add and subtract like terms—terms that have the same variables raised to the same powers.

What is the value of z if $3z + 4z + 7z = -42$?

In this case, the terms all have the same variable and are all to the same power. Thus, we can combine them to get $14z = -42$.

Now we'll divide each side by 14 and get $z = -3$.

To solve a proportion, cross-multiply:

$$\frac{3}{x} = \frac{1}{2}$$
$$x = 6$$

Remember that you can't cancel across an equals sign!

QUICK QUIZ #1

EASY

3. If $\dfrac{3x}{5} = \dfrac{x+2}{3}$, what is the value of x ?

    (A) $\dfrac{1}{2}$

    (B) 1

    (C) 2

    (D) $2\dfrac{1}{2}$

    (E) 3

MEDIUM

6. If $\dfrac{5}{x} = \dfrac{y}{10}$ and $x - y = y$, then $y + x =$

    (A) 5
    (B) 10
    (C) 15
    (D) 25
    (E) 50

HARD

15. If 40 percent of x is equal to 160 percent of y, what is the value of $\dfrac{x}{y}$?

    (A) $\dfrac{1}{12}$

    (B) $\dfrac{1}{4}$

    (C) 4

    (D) 12

    (E) 20

Answers and Explanations: Quick Quiz #1

3. **D** Cross-multiply, and you get $9x = 5(x + 2)$

$$9x = 5x + 10$$

$$4x = 10$$

$$x = 2\frac{1}{2}$$

6. **C** Plug in 10 for x and 5 for y. Both equations are satisfied by those numbers. So $y + x = 15$.

Just to show you the kind of algebra that you'd be forced to do if you didn't plug in—first, cross-multiply to get $xy = 50$. Your other equation is $x - y = y$, so $x = 2y$. Substitute that x into the first equation, and you get $2y^2 = 50$, or $y^2 = 25$. So $y = 5$. Substitute $y = 5$ into either equation and solve for x. You get $x = 10$. Now add them up and you get $x + y = 15$. A lot more work, huh? If you don't plug in when you can, it's really going to slow you down. And that's the least of it. You're also more likely to get the question wrong because the algebra takes so many steps.

15. **C** Although you can plug in for one of the variables and solve for the other, you may find it easier to translate English into Math, and then isolate the two variables. As *percent* means "over 100," *of* means "times," and *is equal to* means "equals," the expression can be rewritten as follows:

$$\frac{40}{100} \times x = \frac{160}{100} \times y$$

Reduce the two fractions:

$$\frac{2}{5} \bullet x = \frac{8}{5} \bullet y$$

Now, isolate the variables on one side of the equation and the numbers on the other side. So, divide both sides by y, and multiply both side by $\frac{5}{2}$:

$$\frac{x}{y} = \frac{8}{5} \times \frac{5}{2} = \frac{8}{2} = 4$$

QUADRATIC EQUATIONS

Even the name is scary. What does it mean, anyway? No matter. All you need to know are a few simple things: factoring and recognizing perfect squares.

To factor, first draw a pair of empty parentheses. Deal with the first term, then the signs, then the last term. For example:

$$x^2 + x - 12 \qquad (\quad)(\quad)$$
$$(x \quad)(x \quad) \ldots \text{first term}$$
$$(x + \quad)(x - \quad) \ldots \text{signs}$$
$$(x + 4)(x - 3) \ldots \text{last term}$$

Check your factoring by multiplying the terms:

first term = $x \cdot x = x^2$

inner term = $4x$

outer term = $-3x$

last term = $4 \times -3 = -12$

Then add them up:

$$x^2 + 4x + -3x + -12 = x^2 + x - 12$$

Some guidelines:

If the last term is positive, your signs will be either +, + or −, −.

If the last term is negative, your signs will be +, −.

Your first try may not be right—don't be afraid to mess around with it a little.

To recognize the difference of two squares, memorize the following:

$$(x + y)(x - y) = x^2 - y^2$$

This format works whether you have variables, as above, or numbers:

$$57^2 - 43^2 = (57 + 43)(57 - 43) = 100 \times 14 = 1400$$

One more thing—memorize the following:

$$(x + y)^2 = (x + y)(x + y) = x^2 + 2xy + y^2$$
$$(x - y)^2 = (x - y)(x - y) = x^2 - 2xy + y^2$$

> **When you see anything that looks like one form of these expressions, try converting to its other form. That should lead you straight to the correct answer.**

QUICK QUIZ #2

EASY

7. If $\dfrac{x^2 + 5x + 6}{x+2} = 12$, then $x =$

   (A) −2
   (B) 2
   (C) 3
   (D) 6
   (E) 9

MEDIUM

15. If $a - b = 3$ and $a^2 - b^2 = 21$, then $a =$

    (A) −3
    (B) −2
    (C) 2
    (D) 5
    (E) 7

HARD

20. If $x < 0$ and $(2x - 1)^2 = 25$, then $x^2 =$

    (A) −4
    (B) −2
    (C) 3
    (D) 4
    (E) 9

Answers and Explanations: Quick Quiz #2

7. **E** First, factor the expression to $(x + 3)(x + 2)$. Now you have

$$\frac{(x+3)(x+2)}{x+2} = 12.$$ The $(x + 2)$ cancels, and you have $x + 3 = 12$, so

$x = 9$. Or you could plug in: If $x = 9$, $\dfrac{9^2 + 5(9) + 6}{9+2} = 12$, or $\dfrac{132}{11} = 12$.

It looks funny, but it works.

15. **D** Factor $a^2 - b^2$ to equal $(a + b)(a - b) = 21$. If $a - b = 3$, then $a + b = 7$. Here you could do one of two things. You can try some different numbers and see what satisfies both simple equations, or you could add the two equations together and get $2a = 10$, $a = 5$.

20. **D** Lots of algebra:

$$(2x - 1)^2 = 25$$

$$(2x - 1)(2x - 1) = 25$$

$$4x^2 - 4x + 1 = 25$$

$$4x^2 - 4x - 24 = 0$$

$$x^2 - x - 6 = 0$$

$$(x - 3)(x + 2) = 0$$

So x can be 3 or -2. If x is negative, it has to be -2, and $-2^2 = 4$. You could also Plug in, but you have to remember that the question asks for x^2, not x. That means (D) and (E) are good answers to try, since they're squares.

Don't forget that one of your main jobs on the SAT is following directions. If you picked (B) or (C), we suspect you did most of the problem correctly but forgot that x is negative, or failed to square x. Don't let carelessness rob you of your hard-earned points!

SIMULTANEOUS EQUATIONS

Two different equations, two different variables. You will not usually have to solve for both variables.

To solve simultaneous equations, stack 'em up, and either add or subtract:

If $2x + 3y = 12$ and $3x - 3y = -2$, what is the value of x?

$$
\begin{array}{r}
2x + 3y = 12 \\
+\ 3x - 3y = -2 \\
\hline
5x = 10 \\
x = 2
\end{array}
$$

If we had subtracted, we'd have gotten $-x + 6y = 14$, which wouldn't get us anywhere. If you choose the wrong operation, no big deal, just try the other one.

> **Don't automatically start solving for x and y—you may not need to. Focus on what the question is specifically asking.**

QUICK QUIZ #3

MEDIUM

9. If $3x + 3y = 4$ and $2x - 3y = 1$, what is the value of x?

    (A) $\dfrac{1}{3}$

    (B) 1

    (C) 3

    (D) 5

    (E) 6

11. If $3x + 5y = 15$ and $x - 2y = 10$, then
$2x + 7y =$

(A) 5
(B) 10
(C) 15
(D) 25
(E) 50

Answers and Explanations: Quick Quiz #3

9. **B** Stack 'em and add:

$$
\begin{array}{r}
3x + 3y = 4 \\
+\ 2x - 3y = 1 \\
\hline
5x \qquad = 5 \\
x = 1
\end{array}
$$

11. **A** Stack 'em and subtract:
$$
\begin{array}{r}
3x + 5y = 15 \\
-(x - 2y = 10) \\
\hline
\end{array}
\qquad
\begin{array}{r}
3x + 5y = 15 \\
-\ x - 2y = -10 \\
\hline
2x + 7y = 5
\end{array}
$$

That's it. You don't have to solve for x or y individually. Less work is good. (Be careful with the signs when you subtract one equation from another.)

INEQUALITIES

Treat these just like equations, but remember one rule: **If you multiply or divide by a negative number, the sign changes direction**.

$$x + 6 > 10 \qquad\qquad 2x > 16 \qquad\qquad -2x > 16$$
$$x > 4 \qquad\qquad\qquad x > 8 \qquad\qquad\quad x < -8$$

It's very easy to mix up the direction of the > or < sign. Be extra careful.

QUICK QUIZ #4

EASY

3. If $3x + 7 < 5x - 4$, then

   (A) $\dfrac{11}{2} < x$

   (B) $x < \dfrac{3}{2}$

   (C) $x < \dfrac{11}{8}$

   (D) $x > \dfrac{2}{3}$

   (E) $\dfrac{11}{2} > x$

MEDIUM

11. If $3b + 8 > 6 + 2b$, and b is a negative integer, then $b =$

    (A) 1
    (B) 0
    (C) −1
    (D) −2
    (E) −3

HARD

20. A "Prime Two Set" is defined as two prime numbers whose difference is 2. For example, 27 and 29 comprise a Prime Two Set, because the difference between them is 2. If p and q comprise a Prime Two Set, which one of the following must be true about p and q ?

   I. The product of the two numbers is an odd number.
  II. $3p$ and $3q$ comprise a Prime Two Set.
 III. The difference between the squares of p and q is 2.

(A) None
(B) I only
(C) I and II only
(D) II and III only
(E) I and III only

ANSWERS AND EXPLANATIONS: QUICK QUIZ #4

3. **A** Treat the inequality just like an equation—subtract $3x$ from both sides, and you get $7 < 2x - 4$. Add 4 to both sides, and you get $11 < 2x$. Divide through by 2, which leaves you with $\frac{11}{2} < x$.

11. **C** Move the bs to one side and the integers to the other, and you get $b > -2$. If b is a negative integer, the only possibility is -1.

20. **B** As there are variables in the answer choices, plug in. Pick an easier Prime Two Set, such as 3 and 5. Roman I is true. While that does not prove it must be true, hang on to it for now. Roman II is false, as 9 and 15 are not prime, nor is their difference 2. Eliminate (C) and (D). Roman III is also false, as the difference between 9 and 25 is not 2. Eliminate (E). Now try one more Prime Two Set to ensure that Roman I is always true. 11 and 13 will work. The product is still odd. It always will be, as a Prime Two Set contains two odd numbers. Eliminate (A).

FUNCTIONS

Functions come in many forms on the SAT, but all of them require you to follow directions.

ETS may make up a math term you've never heard before. Relax, you didn't miss anything exciting in algebra class. Just follow the directions given by the definition of the term.

> The "prime component" of an integer is defined as the sum of all the prime factors of that integer. What is the prime component of 39 ?

First, break down 39 into its prime factors, 3 and 13. Next, find the sum: $3 + 13 = 16$. That's all there is to it.

Alternately, ETS may designate a function by using a strange-looking symbol. For example:

> For any integer t, $[t] = t^2 + t$. What is the value of $[4] - [3]$?

Solution: Take $[4]$ first. The direction tells us to square the number, and then add the number, so $4^2 + 4 = 20$. Now do the same for $[3]$. $3^2 + 3 = 12$. So $[4] - [3] = 20 - 12 = 8$.

Finally, ETS may resort to using actual mathematical functions, indicated by the expression $f(x)$.

> If $f(x) = 2x^2 + 4x + 12$, what is the value of $f(4)$?

Don't be distracted by the fancy symbols; just pop the number into the function and crank out the answer. We want the $f(4)$, so wherever there is an x in the function, we'll replace it with a 4.

$$f(4) = 2(4)^2 + 4(4) + 12$$

$$= 2(16) + 16 + 12$$

$$= 60$$

QUICK QUIZ # 5

Easy

4. If $f(x) = 2x^2 + 3$, for which of the following values of x does $f(x) = 21$?

   (A) −9
   (B) −3
   (C) 0
   (D) 1
   (E) 9

Medium

16. If $[a + b] = a^2 - b^2$, then $\dfrac{[x+y]}{x+y} =$

    (A) $x + y$
    (B) $x - y$
    (C) $2x - 2y$
    (D) 1
    (E) $(x + y)^2$

Hard

19. The height of the steam burst of a certain geyser varies with the length of time since the previous steam burst. The longer the time since the last burst, the greater the height of the steam burst. If t is the time in hours since the previous steam burst and H is the height in meters of the steam burst, which of the following could express the relationship of t and H ?

    (A) $H(t) = \dfrac{1}{2}(t - 7)$

    (B) $H(t) = \dfrac{2}{t-7}$

    (C) $H(t) = 2 - (t - 7)$

    (D) $H(t) = 7 - 2t$

    (E) $H(t) = \dfrac{2}{7t}$

4. **B** In this case, plug in answer choices for the value of x, starting with (C). Plugging in 0 for x gives you $f(0) = 2(0)^2 + 3 = 3$. But you want $f(x) = 21$, so eliminate (C). Now try (B): $f(-3) = 21$, so this is the right answer. Alternatively, set $f(x) = 21$, and solve $21 = 2x^2 + 3$.

16. **B** $[x + y] = x^2 - y^2$, which factors to $(x + y)(x - y)$. When you divide, the $(x + y)$ term cancels, and you're left with $x - y$.

19. **A** The relationship is the greater the time, the greater the height. So the correct function is one that yields a greater H as you increase t.

Try plugging in for t in the functions to see which one increases as t increases. Try $t = 10$ and $t = 20$. Only (A) has a greater H for $t = 10$ than it does for $t = 20$. That is $\frac{1}{2}(10 - 7) > \frac{1}{2}(20 - 7)$. The answer is (A).

4
Geometry

You're not going to believe how simple this is—no proofs, no trig, no parabolas. Just a few rules, a couple of formulas, and your common sense. And don't forget about estimating.

DEFINITIONS

arc	part of a circumference
area	the space inside a two-dimensional figure
bisect	cut in two equal parts
chord	a line that goes through a circle, but does not go through the center; it will always be shorter than the diameter
circumference	the distance around a circle
diagonal	a line from one corner of a square to its opposite corner
diameter	a line directly through the center of a circle; the longest line you can draw in a circle
equidistant	exactly in the middle
equilateral	a triangle with three equal sides, therefore three equal angles (60 degrees each)
hypotenuse	the longest leg of a right triangle, opposite the right angle
isosceles	a triangle with two equal sides and two equal angles
parallel	lines that will never intersect (think railroad tracks)
perimeter	the distance around a figure
perpendicular	two lines that intersect to form 90-degree angles
quadrilateral	any four-sided figure
radius	a line from the center of a circle to the edge of the circle (half the diameter)
volume	the space inside a three-dimensional figure

LINES AND ANGLES

A line has 180°, so the angles formed by any cut to your line will add up to 180°:

Two intersecting lines form a pair of **vertical angles,** that are equal:

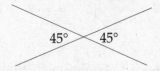

Parallel lines cut by a third line will form two kinds of angles: big ones and little ones. All the big ones are equal to each other; all the little ones are equal to each other. Any big angle plus any little angle will equal 180°:

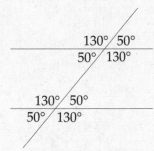

QUICK QUIZ #1

EASY

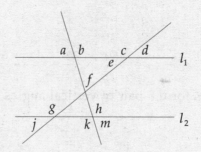

4. In the figure above, l_1 is parallel to l_2. Which of the following angles are NOT equal?

   (A) c and g
   (B) b and h
   (C) a and m
   (D) a and k
   (E) d and j

MEDIUM

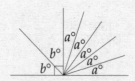

10. In the figure above, what is the value of $4a - b$?

    (A) 18°
    (B) 27°
    (C) 45°
    (D) 54°
    (E) 115°

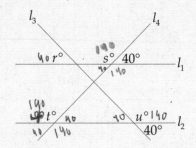

Note: Figure not drawn to scale.

18. Which of the following must be true?

(A) $l_1 \mid \mid l_2$
(B) l_3 bisects l_4
(C) $r = 40°$
(D) $s = t$
(E) $u = 140°$

ANSWERS AND EXPLANATIONS: QUICK QUIZ #1

4. **D** Start with (A) and cross off as you go along. In (D), $a = m$, not k. Keep in mind that the two lines cutting through l_1 and l_2 aren't parallel, and so the angles made by one line have no relationship to the angles made by the other line.

10. **B** Estimate first. Outline the measurement of four of the a's. That's about 60. Now pretend you are subtracting b, about 45. How much is left? Not so much, right? Cross out (D) and (E). Now do the math: $2b = 90°$, so $b = 45°$. $5a = 90$, so $a = 18°$. Now plug those numbers into the equation: $4(18) - 45 = 27$.

18. **E** This question is actually very easy, as long as you don't pick the first answer that looks halfway decent and not even get to (E). Angle u has to be 140° because it's on a straight line with the angle marked 40°. All the other answers look like they're true, but you can't know for certain. The only thing you know for sure is that angles on the same line add up to 180°, and vertical angles are equal. None of these lines are necessarily parallel, so you can't assume anything else.

TRIANGLES

Triangles have 180°.

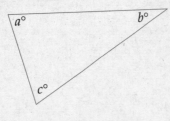

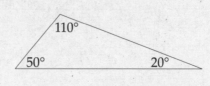

$$a + b + c = 180°$$

$$50° + 20° + 110° = 180°$$

Area $= \frac{1}{2} bh$.

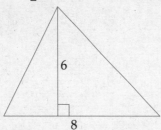

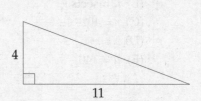

$$\text{area} = \frac{1}{2}(8)(6) = 24$$

$$\text{area} = \frac{1}{2}(11)(4) = 22$$

Perimeter: Add up the sides.

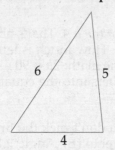

$$\text{Perimeter} = 15$$

Right triangles have a right, or 90°, angle:

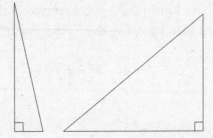

Isosceles triangles have two equal sides and two equal angles:

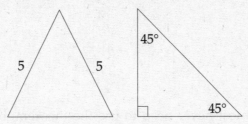

Equilateral triangles have three equal sides and three equal angles:

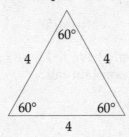

Similar triangles have equal angles and proportional sides:

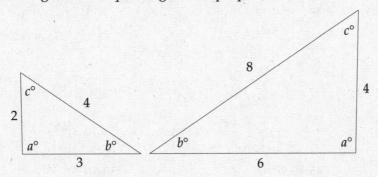

THE WONDERFUL WORLD OF RIGHT TRIANGLES

For any right triangle, if you know the lengths of two of the sides, you can figure out the length of the third side by using the Pythagorean theorem:

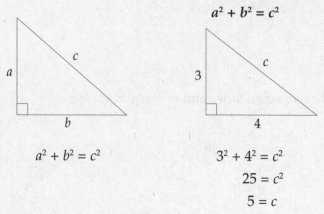

$$a^2 + b^2 = c^2$$

$$a^2 + b^2 = c^2 \qquad\qquad 3^2 + 4^2 = c^2$$
$$25 = c^2$$
$$5 = c$$

However, you almost never need to use the theorem, because almost every right angle you will find will have lengths that fit one of these common Pythagorean triples.

3:4:5   6:8:10   5:12:13

In two special cases, you only have to know one side to figure out the other two, because the sides are in a constant ratio.

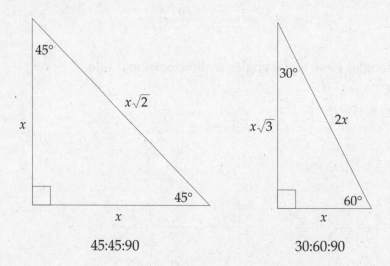

45:45:90   30:60:90

> A 45:45:90 triangle is half of a square, and a 30:60:90 triangle is half of an equilateral triangle.

QUICK QUIZ #2

EASY

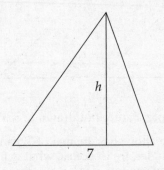

5. If the triangle above has an area of 21, then *h* equals

(A) 3
(B) 4
(C) 6
(D) 7
(E) 8

MEDIUM

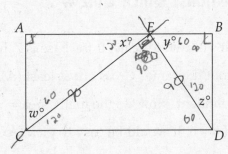

14. If *ABCD* is a rectangle, what is the value of $w + x + y + z$?

(A)   90
(B)   150
(C)   180
(D)   190
(E)   210

HARD

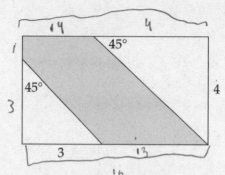

Note: Figure not drawn to scale.

20. If the rectangle above has an area of 32, and the unshaded triangles are isosceles, what is the perimeter of the shaded area?

(A) 16
(B) $10 + 7\sqrt{2}$
(C) $10 + 12\sqrt{2}$
(D) 32
(E) $70\sqrt{2}$

ANSWERS AND EXPLANATIONS: QUICK QUIZ #2

5. **C** Estimate first—it's drawn to scale. If the base is 7, how long does the height look? About the same? Cross out at least (A) and (E), and (B) if you're feeling confident. Now do the math: area = $\frac{1}{2}$ bh, so $\frac{1}{2}$ $(7h) = 21$, and $h = 6$. It would be easy to pick (A) if you weren't paying attention, because $7 \times 3 = 21$, and so it seems appealing.

14. **C** If you picked (A) or (E), you didn't estimate. See how the rectangle is cut up into three triangles? Each of those triangles has 180°. Both of the triangles with marked angles also have right angles because they're corners of a rectangle. So $\triangle ACE + \triangle EBD = 360°$. Subtract the two right angles, and you're left with 180°.

20. **B** First write in everything you know: If the area is 32, the length is 8. That means the base is $3 + 5$ and the left side is $1 + 3$. The triangles in opposing corners are both 45:45:90 triangles: The one on the base has a hypotenuse of $3\sqrt{2}$, and the one with sides of 4 has a hypotenuse of $4\sqrt{2}$. Add up all the sides of the shaded part, and you get $10 + 7\sqrt{2}$.

Here's how it should look:

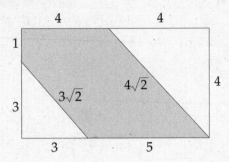

CIRCLES

Circles have 360°. Area = πr^2.

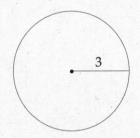

Circumference = $2\pi r$

$r = 3$

$C = 2\pi(3) = 6\pi$

$A = \pi(3)^2 = 9\pi$

> **For any pie slice of a circle, the central angle, arc, and area are in proportion to the whole circle.**

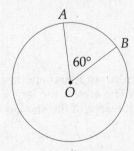

$\dfrac{60°}{360°} = \dfrac{1}{6}$, so arc AB is $\dfrac{1}{6}$ of the circumference, and pie slice AOB is $\dfrac{1}{6}$ of the total area.

QUICK QUIZ #4

EASY

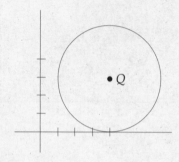

4. Center *Q* of the circle above has coordinates of (4, 3). What is the circumference of the circle?

   (A) π
   (B) 2π
   (C) 6π
   (D) 8π
   (E) 9π

MEDIUM

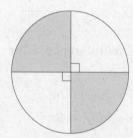

13. If the circumference of the circle above is 16π, what is the total area of the shaded regions?

    (A) 64π
    (B) 32π
    (C) 12π
    (D) 8π
    (E) 4π

HARD

20. One circle has a radius of *r*, and another circle has a radius of 2*r*. The area of the larger circle is how many times the area of the smaller circle?

    (A) .5
    (B) 1.5
    (C) 2
    (D) 3
    (E) 4

4. **C** The easiest way to solve this is simply to count the number of units in the radius, which is 3. Make sure you draw a radius on the diagram—if you draw it perpendicular to the y-axis you'll be able to count the units with no problem. If you picked (E), you found the area. Read the question carefully and give 'em what they ask for.

13. **B** The circumference is 16 , so use the circumference formula to get the radius: $2\pi r = 16\pi$, and $r = 8$. The area of the whole circle is $\pi r^2 = \pi(8)^2 = 64\pi$. Hold on—don't pick (A). At this point, you could happily estimate the shaded area as half the circle and pick (B). (Nothing else is close.) In fact, the shaded area is exactly half of the circle because each marked angle is 90°, which makes each of those pie slices $\frac{90°}{360°}$ or $\frac{1}{4}$ of the circle. So two of them make up $\frac{1}{2}$ of the circle, or 32π. Trust what your eyes tell you.

20. **E** Plug in. If $r = 2$, then the area of the small circle is 4π. The radius of the second circle is 2(2) or 4, so the area is 16π. The larger circle is 4 times as big as the smaller circle. (Don't you just love to plug in?)

> **Notice how the hard question doesn't give you a picture or any real numbers to use. So draw the picture and make up your own numbers. Try to visualize the problem. Plugging In works just as well on geometry problems as it does on algebra problems.**

Note: A very common careless error on circle problems is getting the area and circumference mixed up. Don't worry! The formulas are printed on the first page of each math section in case you forgot them.

QUADRILATERALS

Quadrilaterals have 360°.

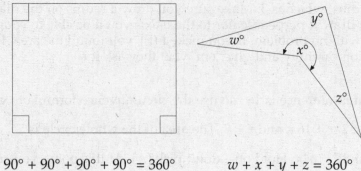

$$90° + 90° + 90° + 90° = 360°$$ $$w + x + y + z = 360°$$

Perimeter: Add up the sides.

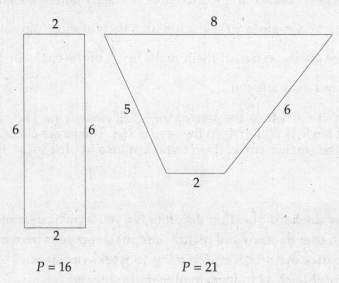

$$P = 16$$ $$P = 21$$

PARALLELOGRAMS

Parallelograms have two pairs of parallel lines, but no right angles.

Area = Base × Height

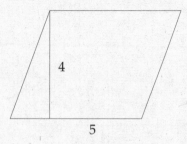

$$A = bh \qquad A = (5)(4) \qquad A = 20$$

Rectangles have four 90° angles and two pairs of parallel lines.

Area = $l \times w$

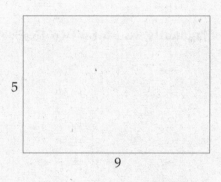

$$A = lw$$
$$A = (9)(5)$$
$$A = 45$$

Note that there's no relationship between the perimeter of a rectangle and its area.

$$P = 36 \qquad\qquad P = 36$$
$$A = 17 \qquad\qquad A = 81$$

Squares have four 90° angles and two pairs of parallel lines, all the same length.

Area = $l \times w$ or s^2

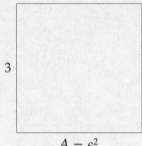

$A = s^2$
$A = 3^2$
$A = 9$

If you cut a square diagonally, you form two 45:45:90 triangles.

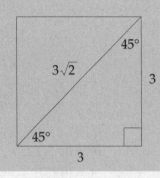

QUICK QUIZ #5

Easy

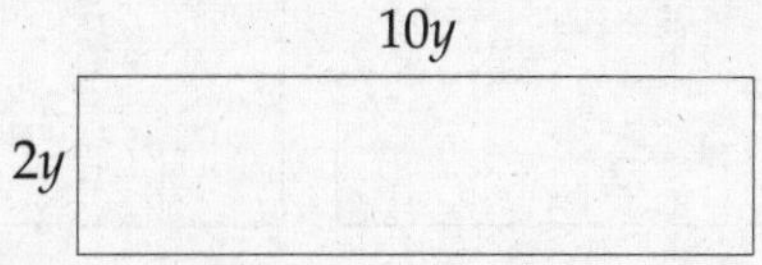

```
           10y
      ┌──────────────────┐
  2y  │                  │
      └──────────────────┘
```

3. If $y = 3$, what is the perimeter of the figure above?

    (A) 12
    (B) 20
    (C) 50
    (D) 60
    (E) 72

Medium

9. What is the area of a square with a diagonal 5 ?

    (A) 10

    (B) 12.5

    (C) 25

    (D) $25\sqrt{2}$

    (E) $50\sqrt{2}$

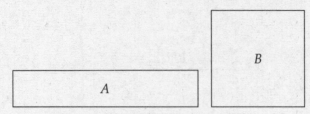

Note: Figures not drawn to scale.

12. The length of Rectangle A is $\frac{1}{3}$ the length of Rectangle B, and the width of A is twice the width of B. What is the ratio of the area of A to the area of B ?

(A) $\frac{1}{3}$

(B) $\frac{2}{3}$

(C) 1

(D) $\frac{3}{2}$

(E) $\frac{3}{4}$

ANSWERS AND EXPLANATIONS: QUICK QUIZ #25

3. **E** Figure out the dimensions of the rectangle if $y = 3$. That makes the length $10 \times 3 = 30$, and the width $2 \times 3 = 6$. Write those numbers on the diagram where they belong. To get the perimeter, add up all the sides. $30 + 30 + 6 + 6 = 72$.

9. **B** If the square has diagonal 5, then 5 is also the hypotenuse of the two 45:45:90 right triangles that are formed by the diagonal. Since you know the hypotenuse, you can find the other sides of the triangle, which are the sides of the square. As you know, in a 45:45:90 triangle, the ratio of the sides is $x:x:x\sqrt{2}$. Since the diagonal is 5, you know that $x\sqrt{2} = 5$, so the side $x = \frac{5}{\sqrt{2}}$. The area of the square is therefore $\frac{5}{\sqrt{2}} \times \frac{5}{\sqrt{2}} = 12.5$.

12. **B** Plug in. If the length of A is $\frac{1}{3}$ the length of B, make the length of

$B = 6$ and the length of $A = 2$. If the width of A is twice the width of B,

make the width of $B = 4$ and the width of $A = 8$. Now the area of

$A = 2 \times 8 = 16$, and the area of B is $6 \times 4 = 24$. $\frac{A}{B}$ is $\frac{16}{24}$, or $\frac{2}{3}$.

BOXES AND CANS

Forget spheres, cones, and other complicated 3-D nightmares. Most often, you will be asked only to deal with rectangular solids (boxes), cubes (square boxes), and possibly cylinders (cans).

No matter what the shape is, the volume equals the area of one face × the third dimension (the depth or the height). Here are the formulas you need to know:

Rectangular Box

Volume = $l \times w \times h$

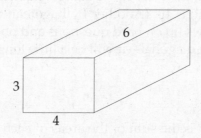

$$V = lwh$$
$$V = 6(3)(4)$$
$$V = 72$$

Cube

Volume = s^3

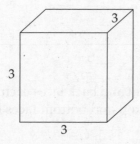

$$V = s^3$$
$$V = 3^3$$
$$V = 27$$

To find the diagonal of a box, draw in two right triangles: one on the end of the box and the other cutting through the box. The second triangle will have the hypotenuse of the first triangle as its base, the length of the box as its height, and the diagonal of the box as its hypotenuse. Here's how it will look:

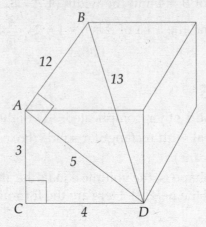

If *AC* is 3 and *DC* is 4, then *AD* is 5 (Pythagorean triple). If *AD* is 5 and *AB* is 12, then *BD* (the diagonal) is 13. (Another Pythagorean triple.) As you can probably guess, this only shows up on hard questions and not that often. You can also estimate the length of the diagonal—it will be a little longer than the longest edge of the box.

SURFACE AREA

The surface area of a box is the sum of the areas of each of the faces.

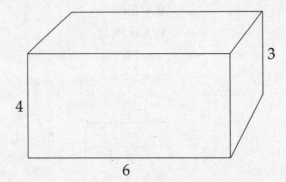

In the figure above, the front and back faces each measure 6 by 4; the side faces each measure 4 by 3; and the top and bottom faces each measure 6 by 3.

Front face $(6 \times 4) = 24$

Back face $(6 \times 4) = 24$

Left face $(4 \times 3) = 12$

Right face $(4 \times 3) = 12$

Top face $(6 \times 3) = 18$

Bottom face $(6 \times 3) = 18$

The surface area is the sum of these faces. $24 + 24 + 12 + 12 + 18 + 18 = 108$.

Cylinder

Volume = r^2h

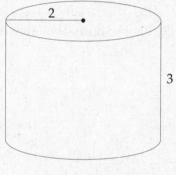

$V = r^2h$

$V = 2^2(3)$

$V = 12$

If the problem concerns a cone, pyramid, or any shape other than the ones described above, the necessary formula will be given in the question. If you aren't given a formula, you don't need one.

QUICK QUIZ #6

EASY

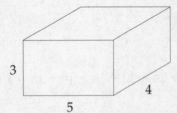 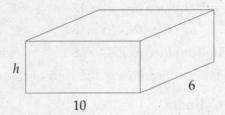

Note: Figures not drawn to scale.

6. If the volumes of the two boxes above are equal, then *h* equals

   (A) 1
   (B) 2
   (C) 4
   (D) 5
   (E) 20

MEDIUM

9. Sam is packing toy blocks into a crate. If each block is a cube with a side of 6 inches, and the crate is 1 foot high, 2 feet long, and 2 feet wide, how many blocks can Sam fit into the crate?

   (A) 6
   (B) 12
   (C) 24
   (D) 32
   (E) 40

HARD

12. The surface area of a rectangular solid measuring 5 × 6 × 8 is how much greater than the surface area of a rectangular solid measuring 3 × 6 × 8 ?

   (A) 12
   (B) 24
   (C) 48
   (D) 56
   (E) 96

ANSWERS AND EXPLANATIONS: QUICK QUIZ #6

6. **A** The box on the left has volume = 3 × 4 × 5 = 60. The box on the right is then 10 × 6 × h = 60. So h = 1. Don't forget to estimate!

9. **D** First draw the crate. It should look like this:

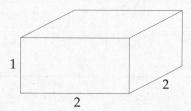

Now visualize putting blocks into the crate. If the blocks are 6 inches high, you'll be able to stack 2 rows in the crate since the crate is a foot high. Now mark off 6-inch intervals along the side of the crate. (You're dividing 2 feet, or 24 inches, by 6 inches.) You can fit 4 blocks along each side. Now multiply everything together and you get 2 × 4 × 4 = 32 blocks.

You can also divide the volume of the crate by the volume of each block, as long as your units are consistent:

$$\frac{1 \text{ ft} \times 2 \text{ ft} \times 2 \text{ ft}}{\frac{1}{2} \text{ ft} \times \frac{1}{2} \text{ ft} \times \frac{1}{2} \text{ ft}} \quad \text{or} \quad \frac{12 \text{ in} \times 24 \text{ in} \times 24 \text{ in}}{6 \text{ in} \times 6 \text{ in} \times 6 \text{ in}}$$

12. **D** Find the surface area of the first figure. It has two sides 5 × 6, two sides 6 × 8, and two sides 5 × 8. Therefore its surface area is 30 + 30 + 48 + 48 + 40 + 40, which makes 236. The second figure has two sides 3 × 6, two sides 6   8, and two sides 3 × 8. Its surface area is 18 + 18 + 48 + 48 + 24 + 24, or 180. The difference between these two surface areas is 56.

COORDINATE GEOMETRY

Remember how to plot points? The first number is *x* and the second is *y*.

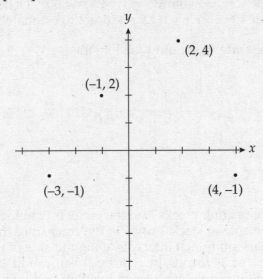

To find the length of a horizontal or vertical line, count the units:

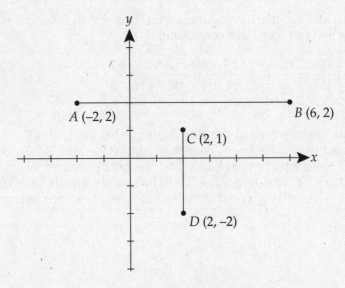

AB = 8 and *CD* = 3

To find the length of any other line, draw in a right triangle and use the Pythagorean theorem:

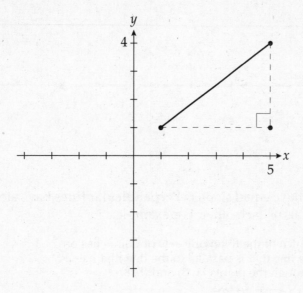

The triangle has legs of 3 and 4, so $3^2 + 4^2 = c^2$, and $c = 5$. (It's a Pythagorean triple again.)

To find the slope, put the rise over the run. The formula is

$$\text{slope} = \frac{y_1 - y_2}{x_1 - x_2}$$

It doesn't matter which point you begin with, just be consistent.

What is the slope of the line containing points (2, –3) and (4, 3)?

$$\text{slope} = \frac{-3 - 3}{2 - 4} = \frac{-6}{-2} = 3 \text{ or } \frac{3 - (-3)}{4 - 2} = \frac{6}{2} = 3$$

A slope that goes from low to high is positive.

A slope that goes from high to low is negative.

A slope that goes straight across is 0.

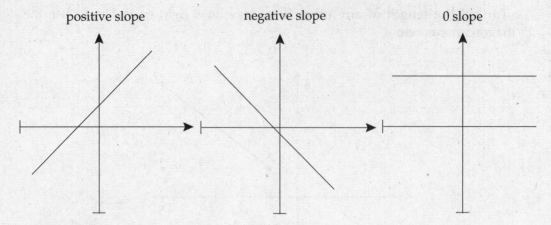

positive slope   negative slope   0 slope

Parallel lines have equal slopes. **Perpendicular lines** have slopes that are negative reciprocals of each other. For example:

> Which of the following sets of points lies on the line that is parallel to the line that passes through the points (1, 3) and (5, 8) ?
>
> (A) (–5, –8), (1, 3)
> (B) (12, 2), (8, –3)
> (C) (5, 3), (1,8)
> (D) (15, 3), (6, 2)
> (E) (–7, –5), (2, 3)

First, find the slope of the first set of points.

$$\text{slope} = \frac{3-8}{1-5} = \frac{-5}{-4} = \frac{5}{4}$$

Then check the answer choices and look for the set of points that has an equal slope. The correct answer is (B).

Try the same thing with perpendicular lines.

> Which of the following sets of points lies on the line that is perpendicular to the line that passes through the points (1, 3) and (5, 8) ?
>
> (A) (16, 7), (11, 11)
> (B) (8, 5), (3, 1)
> (C) (2, 5), (3, 13)
> (D) (7, 8), (5, 11)
> (E) (3, 3), (8, 8)

We already found the slope. Now we need its negative reciprocal, which is $\frac{-4}{5}$. Check the answers. Answer choice (A) gives us:

$$\text{slope} = \frac{7-11}{16-11} = \frac{-4}{5}$$

Bingo!

QUICK QUIZ #7

EASY

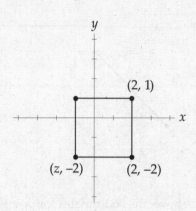

4. If the figure above is a square, what is the value of z ?

(A) −2
(B) −1
(C) 1
(D) 2
(E) 4

MEDIUM

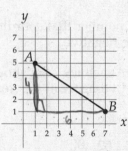

14. In the figure above, what is the length of AB ?

(A) 4

(B) $2\sqrt{6}$

(C) 7

(D) $\sqrt{52}$

(E) $\sqrt{63}$

HARD

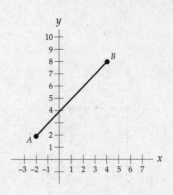

19. In the figure above, the coordinates for point A are $(-2, 2)$ and the coordinates for point B are $(4, 8)$. If line CD, not shown, is parallel to the line AB, what is the slope of line CD?

    (A) -1
    (B) 0
    (C) 1
    (D) 2
    (E) 4

ANSWERS AND EXPLANATIONS: QUICK QUIZ #7

4. **B** Just count the units. Remember that coordinates in the lower left quadrant will always be negative.

14. **D** Use the units to measure each leg. You should get one leg = 4 and the other = 6. Now use the Pythagorean theorem: $4^2 + 6^2 = c^2$.

$$16 + 36 = c^2$$

$$52 = c^2$$

$$\sqrt{52} = c$$

19. **C** Write in the coordinates of A and B. $A = (-2, 2)$ and $B = (4, 8)$. So the slope of $AB = \dfrac{2-8}{2-4} = \dfrac{-6}{-6} = 1$. If CD is parallel to AB, it has the same slope. (You could draw in a parallel line and recalculate the slope, but you'd be doing extra work.)

CHARTS AND GRAPHS

The key to chart questions is to take a moment to size up the chart before you attack the question. Pay particular attention to what units are used.

Number of Dogs Washed by Deidre's Dog Wash

= 100 dogs

Above is a chart representing how many dogs were washed by Deirdre's Dog Wash in the first half of 2004. Which month features the greatest percent increase of the number of dogs washed over the previous month?

(A) February
(B) March
(C) April
(D) May
(E) June

First, note the units. Each dog shape represents 100 dogs. Now, attack the question. You need to find the percent increase, which you'll recall is the difference between two numbers divided by the original number. (A) and (D) both show a decrease in the number of dogs, so eliminate them. In March, 400 dogs were washed, while 200 dogs were washed in the previous month. Using our percent increase formula, we get

$$\frac{\text{difference}}{\text{original}} = \frac{400 - 200}{200} = \frac{200}{200} = 100\%$$

None of the other choices is even close, so (B) is our answer.

For graphs involving functions, you will sometimes be asked to provide info on a portion of a function or how one function was translated into another function.

Consider the following function $f(x)$, with x values of a and b, as indicated:

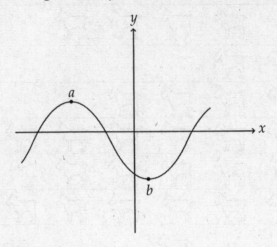

At $x < a$, $f(x)$ is rising

At $a < x < b$, $f(x)$ is falling

At $b < x$, $f(x)$ is rising again

If a new function, $g(x)$, is formed by moving our original function $f(x)$, $g(x)$ would be defined as follows:

If $f(x)$ is moved 4 units up the y axis, then $g(x) = f(x) + 4$

If $f(x)$ is moved 5 units down the y axis, then $g(x) = f(x) - 5$

If $f(x)$ is moved 2 units to the right along the x axis, then $g(x) = f(x - 2)$

If $f(x)$ is moved 3 units up the y axis, then $g(x) = f(x + 3)$

QUICK QUIZ #8

EASY

Adore-a-Bubble Soda Company's Sales

Flavor	1980	2000
Snappy Apple	50%	50%
Raspberry Rush	25%	5%
Fresh Fizz	10%	12%
Cranberry Crackle	12%	10%
Purple Pop	3%	3%
Total	100%	100%

6. The table above shows the Adore-a-Bubble Soda Company's sales for 1980 and 2000. The company sold 200 trillion cans of soda in 1980. If the company sold 40 trillion more cans of soda in 2000 than it did in 1980, then for which flavor did the <u>number</u> of cans of soda sold increase by 20% from 1980 to 2000 ?

(A) Snappy Apple
(B) Raspberry Rush
(C) Fresh Fizz
(D) Cranberry Crackle
(E) Purple Pop

MEDIUM

t	−1	0	1	2
$g(t)$	0	−2	0	6

11. The table above provides values for the function g for selected values of t. Which of the following defines the function g ?

(A) $g(t) = t^2 - 2$
(B) $g(t) = t^2 + 2$
(C) $g(t) = 2t^2 - 2$
(D) $g(t) = 2t^2 + 2$
(E) $g(t) = t^2 + 6$

HARD

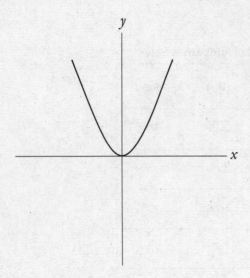

18. The quadratic function $y = f(x)$ is shown above. Which of the following graphs represents the function $y = f(x + 3) - 4$?

(A)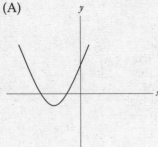

(B)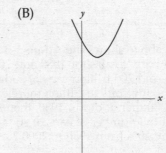

(C)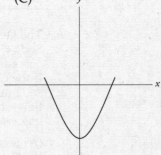

(D)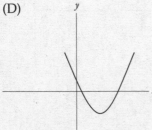

(E)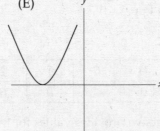

ANSWERS AND EXPLANATIONS: QUICK QUIZ #8

6. **A** Use percent translation and the percent increase/decrease formula.

For example, the number of cans of Snappy Apple sold in 1980 is 50% of 200 trillion. Using translation, you get $\frac{50}{100} \times 200$ trillion $= \frac{1}{2} \times 200$ trillion = 100 trillion. In 2000, the company sold 50% of 240 trillion.

Using translation again gives you 120 trillion. Now you need to find the percent increase using the formula:

$$\text{Percent increase} = \frac{Difference}{Original} \times 100$$

Plugging in the values you found above gives you $\frac{120 \text{ trillion} - 100 \text{ trillion}}{100 \text{ trillion}} \times 100 = \frac{1}{5} \times 100 = 20$. This means that sales of Snappy Apple increased by 20%, so (A) is the correct answer.

11. **C** Plug the values in the chart into the answer choices. Start with the easiest value for t, namely 0. Because when t is 0, $g(t)$ is –2, eliminate (B), (D), and (E). Now check $t = 1$, which should yield $g(t) = 0$. Eliminate (A). (C) is the answer.

18. **A** Don't worry about actual numbers here—just how the graph moves. The – 4 outside of the parentheses moves the function down, so eliminate any answer choices that do not move down. (B) and (E) are wrong. The + 3 inside the parentheses moves the function to the left, so eliminate any remaining answer choices that do not move to the left. (C) and (D) are wrong. Only (A) works.

GEOMETRY: FINAL TIPS AND REMINDERS

- Always estimate first when the figure is drawn to scale.

- Always write the information given on the diagram, including any information you figure out along the way.

- If you don't know how to start, just look and see what shapes are involved. The solution to the problem will come through using the information we've gone over that pertains to that shape.

QUICK QUIZ #9

EASY

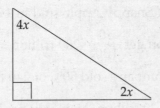

6. In the figure above, $x =$

    (A) 15
    (B) 45
    (C) 85
    (D) 105
    (E) 125

MEDIUM

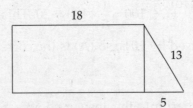

Note: Figure not drawn to scale.

11. The figure above is composed of a rectangle and
     a triangle. What is the perimeter of the figure
     above?

     (A) 49
     (B) 66
     (C) 70
     (D) 93
     (E) 111

HARD

14. What is the slope of a line that is perpendicular to the line that passes through points (1, 2) and (2, 4) ?

    (A) –2

    (B) $-\dfrac{1}{2}$

    (C) 1

    (D) $\dfrac{1}{2}$

    (E) 2

ANSWERS AND EXPLANATIONS: QUICK QUIZ #9

6. **A** Since the angles in a triangle always add up to 180, and you have a right angle, you know that the other two angles must have a sum of 90. You can write the equation: $4x + 2x = 90$. Now you can solve $6x = 90$, so x must be equal to 15.

11. **B** If you remember the ratios that work for the Pythagorean theorem, you'll remember that 5:12:13 is one common set of sides for right triangles on the SAT. Since this right triangle has sides 5 and 13, you know that the height of the triangle (which is also the height of the rectangle) is 12. So to figure out the perimeter of the whole figure, you need to add up the sides: $18 + 12 + 18 + 5 + 13 = 66$.

14. **B** Start by estimating. If you draw the line that passes through (1, 2) and (2, 4), you see that it goes up and to the right, so it has a positive slope. If you draw a line perpendicular to it, the new line will go down and to the right, so it must have negative slope. This means that the answer has to be either (A) or (B). Further, if you drew your diagram accurately, you'll notice that the second line is at a very shallow angle, so its slope must be between –1 and 0, leaving only (B) as the possible answer choice.

5

Grid-In Questions

GRID-INS

Grid-in questions have no answer choices. You must solve the question, write your answer on a grid, and bubble it in. This isn't as bad as it sounds. The order of difficulty applies, so the first three questions (11–13) are easy, the middle four questions (14–17) are medium, and the final three questions (18–20) are hard. Take your time on the easy and medium questions, as always.

TIPS FOR GRID-IN HAPPINESS

- Don't bother to reduce fractions: $\frac{3}{6}$ is as good as $\frac{1}{2}$.

- Don't round off decimals. If your answer has more than four digits, just start to the left of the decimal point and fit in as many as you can.

- Don't grid in mixed fractions. Either convert to one fraction or a decimal. (Use 4.25 or $\frac{17}{4}$, not $4\frac{1}{4}$.)

- If the question asks for "one possible value," any answer that works is okay.

- Forget about negatives, variables, and π. You can't grid them.

- You can still plug in if the question has an implied variable.

QUICK QUIZ #1

EASY

11. What is the value of x ?

MEDIUM

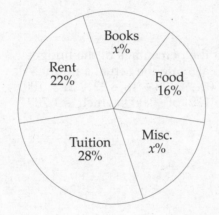

14. The chart above shows Orwell's projected expenditures for his freshman year at River State University. If he plans to spend a total of $10,000 for the year, how many dollars will Orwell spend on books?

HARD

17. If the function $r(s)$ is defined as $2s + 3$ for all values of s, and $r(4) = x$, what is the value of $r(x)$?

Answers and Explanations: Quick Quiz #1

11. **30**

    Since this is a right triangle, the other 2 angles add up to 90. So $3x = 90$ and $x = 30$.

14. **1700**

    Two steps: First figure out the percentage of the budget spent on books, and then calculate the actual amount. All the pie slices add up to 100%, so $28 + 16 + 22 + 2x = 100$. $2x = 34$ and $x = 17\%$. Take 17% of 10,000, which is 1,700.

17. **25**

    When a number is inside the parentheses, plug it into the equation. Thus, $r(4) = 2(4) + 3 = 11$. Thus $x = 11$. The question is not asking for $r(4)$, but $r(x)$. As you know $x = 11$, the question is asking for $r(11)$, so plug 11 into the formula. $r(11) = 2(11) + 3 = 25$.

6
Problem Sets

The following groups of questions were designed for quick, concentrated study. The problems come in groups of ten (three easy, four medium, three hard). Answers and explanations follow immediately. The idea is for you to check your answers right after working the problems so that you can learn from your mistakes before you continue.

Don't simply count up how many you got wrong and then breeze on to the next thing—take a careful look at *how* you got the question wrong. Did you use the wrong strategy? Not remember the necessary basic math? Make a goofy computation error? Write an equation and plug in at the same time?

> **You need to know the cause of your mistakes
> before you can stop making them.**

Here are sets of plugging in, geometry, exponent, and other typical problem types to help you learn how to recognize those types of questions when they come up—so pay attention to the look and feel of them.

One last thing—the question numbers correspond to the difficulty level. For the 20-question multiple-choice section, the easy questions are number 1 to 8, the mediums are number 7 to 14, and the hard ones are number 15 to 20. You must always be aware of the difficulty level of the question you're working on.

PROBLEM SET 1: PLUGGING IN

EASY

1. Sinéad has 4 more than three times the number of hats that Maria has. If Maria has x hats, then in terms of x, how many hats does Sinéad have?

    (A) $3x + 4$
    (B) $3(x + 4)$
    (C) $4(x + 3)$
    (D) $4(3x)$
    (E) $7x$

2. When 6 is subtracted from $10p$, the result is t. Which of the following equations represents the statement above?

    (A) $t = 6(p - 10)$
    (B) $t = 6p - 10$
    (C) $t = 10(6 - p)$
    (D) $10p - 6 = t$
    (E) $10 - 6p = t$

3. Sally scored a total of $4b + 12$ points in a certain basketball game. She scored the same number of points in each of the game's 4 periods. In terms of b, how many points did she score in each period?

    (A) $b - 8$
    (B) $b + 3$
    (C) $b + 12$
    (D) $4b + 3$
    (E) $16b + 48$

MEDIUM

4. If t is a prime number, and x is a factor of 12, then $\dfrac{t}{x}$ could be all of the following EXCEPT

   (A) $\dfrac{1}{12}$

   (B) $\dfrac{1}{4}$

   (C) $\dfrac{1}{2}$

   (D) 1

   (E) 2

5. Roseanne is 6 years younger than Tom will be in 2 years. Roseanne is now x years old. In terms of x, how old was Tom 3 years ago?

   (A) $x - 7$
   (B) $x - 1$
   (C) $x + 1$
   (D) $x + 3$
   (E) $x + 5$

6. A phone company charges 10 cents per minute for the first 3 minutes of a call and $10 - c$ cents for each minute thereafter. What is the cost, in cents, of a 10-minute phone call?

   (A) $200 - 20c$
   (B) $100c + 70$
   (C) $30 + 7c$
   (D) $100 - 7c$
   (E) $100 - 70c$

7. If $0 < pt < 1$, and p is a negative integer, which of the following must be less than -1 ?

   (A) p

   (B) $p - t$

   (C) $t + p$

   (D) $2t$

   (E) $t \times \dfrac{1}{2}$

HARD

8. If x and y are positive integers, and
$\sqrt{x} = y + 3$, then $y^2 =$

(A) $x - 9$
(B) $x + 9$
(C) $x^2 - 9$
(D) $x - 6\sqrt{x} + 9$
(E) $x^2 - 6\sqrt{x} + 9$

9. If cupcakes are on sale at 8 for c cents, and gingerbread squares are on sale at 6 for g cents, what is the cost, in cents, of 2 cupcakes and 1 gingerbread square?

(A) $8c + 3g$

(B) $\dfrac{cg}{3}$

(C) $\dfrac{8c + 6g}{3}$

(D) $\dfrac{8c + 3g}{14}$

(E) $\dfrac{3c + 2g}{12}$

10. If the side of a square is $x + 1$, then the diagonal of the square is

(A) $x^2 + 1$
(B) $2x + 2$
(C) $x\sqrt{2} + \sqrt{2}$
(D) $x^2 + 2$
(E) $\sqrt{2x} + \sqrt{2}$

Answers and Explanations: Problem Set 1

Easy

1. **A** Forget the algebra. Plug in 2 for x, so Maria has 2 hats. Triple that number is 6. Sinéad has 4 more than triple, so Sinéad has $4 + 6 = 10$. You should put a circle around 10, so you can remember it's the answer to the question, the magic number. Now plug 2 into the answer choices. (A) gives us $3(2) + 4 = 10$, which is just what you're looking for.

2. **D** Plug in 2 for p. $2 \times 10 = 20$; $20 - 6 = 14$. So $t = 14$. (Since this is an equation, when you pick one number, the other number is automatically produced by the equation.) If $p = 2$ and $t = 14$, (A) is $14 = 6(2 - 10)$. Does $14 = 12 - 60$? Not on this planet. (D) is $10(2) - 6 = 14$, or $20 - 6 = 14$. The equation works, so that's your answer.

3. **B** Make $b = 2$. That means she scored $4(2) + 12 = 20$ points total. If she scored the same number of points in each of the 4 periods, you have to divide the total by 4, so she scored $20 \div 4 = 5$ points per period. Put a circle around 5. Now on to the answer choices. (A) is $2 - 8$. (B) is $2 + 3 = 5$, which is our magic number.

Notice how we keep plugging in 2? That's because we're trying to make things as easy as possible. To get these questions right, you didn't *have* to pick 2; on some questions, 2 might not work so well. You can pick whatever you want. Just make sure your number doesn't require you to make ugly, unpleasant calculations. *Avoiding hard work* is the name of the game. If the number you pick turns bad on you, pick another one.

Always check all five answers when you plug in, just in case you get two correct answers. In that case, quickly plug in with a new number to find out which one was wrong.

MEDIUM

4. **A** This question is tricky to spot as a plugging in question because the answer choices don't have variables. It does, however, ask how variables relate, so you can still plug in. Make a short list of possibilities for t, starting with the first prime number. Then do the same for x, listing the factors of 12 in pairs.

$$t = 2, 3, 5, 7 \qquad\qquad x = 1, 12, 2, 6, 3, 4$$

The question asks for $\dfrac{t}{x}$, which you can make by putting any number in your t column over any number from your x column. (B) is $\dfrac{3}{12}$. (C) is $\dfrac{3}{6}$. (D) is $\dfrac{2}{2}$. (E) is $\dfrac{2}{1}$. No matter what you do, you can't make $\dfrac{1}{12}$, so (A) is your answer. If you didn't remember that 1 is not prime, you were probably banging your head against a wall. When that happens, go on to the next question.

5. **C** Let $x = 10$, so Roseanne is now 10 years old. That's 6 years younger than 16, so Tom must be 16 in 2 years, which makes him 14 now. The question asks for Tom's age 3 years ago; if he's 14 now, 3 years ago he was 11. Circle 11. In the answer choices, plug 10 in for x. (A) is $10 - 3$. Nope. (B) is $10 - 1$. Nope. (C) is $10 + 1$. Yeah!

6. **D** Let $c = 8$. The first 3 minutes of the call would be $3(10)$, or 30 cents. The remaining minutes would be charged at $10 - 8$ cents, or 2 cents a minute. There are 7 minutes remaining, so $2 \times 7 = 14$. The total cost is $30 + 14 = 44$ cents. On to the answer choices: (A) and (B) are way too big. (C) is $30 + 7(8) = 86$. (D) is $100 - 56 = 44$.

7. **C** First take a good look at $0 < pt < 1$. You know that pt is a positive fraction. If p is a negative integer, then t must be a negative fraction. Now plug in. (Or you can just try numbers until you find some that satisfy the inequality.) Let $p = -1$ and $t = -\frac{1}{2}$. Try them in the answer choices, crossing out any answer that's –1 or higher. (A) is –1, cross it out. (B) is $-\frac{1}{2}$, cross it out. (C) is $-1\frac{1}{2}$, leave it in. (D) is –1, cross it out. (E) is –1, cross it out. The trouble with *must be* questions is that you can only *eliminate* answers by plugging in, you can't simply choose the first answer that works. That's because the answer may work with certain numbers but not with others—and you're looking for an answer that *must be true*, no matter what numbers you pick. These questions can be time-consuming, so if you're running low on time, you may want to skip them.

HARD

8. **D** Let $x = 25$. That makes $y = 2$. The question asks for y^2, and $2^2 = 4$. Circle it. Now try the answer choices. (A) is $25 - 9$. (B) is $25 + 9$. (C) is huge. (D) is $25 - 30 + 9 = 4$. Not so bad, huh?

9. **E** Let $c = 16$ and $g = 12$. That means the cupcakes and the gingerbread squares sell for 2 cents apiece. One gingerbread square and two cupcakes will cost 6 cents. Circle 6. On to the answer choices, plugging in 16 for c and 12 for g. (E) gives you $\frac{3(16)+2(12)}{12} = 6$. Use your calculator for that last part. Get it right? Then go to a bakery and celebrate.

10. **C** Draw yourself a little square and label the sides $x + 1$. Draw in a diagonal. Let $x = 2$. The side of the square is then 3, and the diagonal is $3\sqrt{2}$. (The diagonal is the hypotenuse of a 45:45:90 triangle.) Plug 2 into the answer choices. (C) gives you $2\sqrt{2} + \sqrt{2} = 3\sqrt{2}$.

PROBLEM SET 2: MORE PLUGGING IN

EASY

1. Jim and Pam bought x quarts of ice cream for a party. If 10 people attended the party, including Jim and Pam, and if each person ate the same amount of ice cream, which of the following represents the amount of ice cream, in quarts, eaten by each person at the party?

   (A) $10x$

   (B) $5x$

   (C) x

   (D) $\dfrac{x}{5}$

   (E) $\dfrac{x}{10}$

2. If x and y are integers and $\dfrac{x}{y} = 1$, then $x + y$ must be

   (A) positive
   (B) negative
   (C) odd
   (D) even
   (E) greater than 1

3. If $3x - y = 12$, then $\dfrac{y}{3} =$

   (A) $x - 3$
   (B) $x - 4$
   (C) $3x - 4$
   (D) $9x - 12$
   (E) $3x + 4$

4. When x is divided by 3, the remainder is z. In terms of z, which of the following could be equal to x ?

   (A) $z - 3$
   (B) $3 - z$
   (C) $3z$
   (D) $6 + z$
   (E) $9 + 2z$

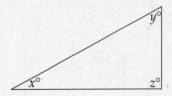

5. In the figure above, $2x = y$. In terms of x, $z =$

   (A) $180 + 2x$
   (B) $180 + x$
   (C) $180 - x$
   (D) $180 - 3x$
   (E) $180 - 4x$

6. If w, x, y, and z are consecutive positive integers, and $w > x > y > z$, which of the following CANNOT be true?

   (A) $x + z = w$
   (B) $y + z = x$
   (C) $x - y = z$
   (D) $w - x = y$
   (E) $w - z = y$

7. The volume of a certain rectangular solid is $12x$. If the dimensions of the solid are the integers x, y, and z, what is the greatest possible value of z ?

   (A) 36
   (B) 24
   (C) 12
   (D) 6
   (E) 4

8. If $x^3 < 0 < xy^2z$, which of the following must be true?

   I. xyz is positive
   II. $x^2y^2z^3$ is positive
   III. $x^3y^2z^3$ is positive

   (A) I only
   (B) III only
   (C) I and II only
   (D) II and III only
   (E) I, II, and III

9. When a is divided by 7, the remainder is 4. When b is divided by 3, the remainder is 2. If $0 < a < 24$ and $2 < b < 8$, which of the following could have a remainder of 0 when divided by 8 ?

   (A) $\dfrac{a}{b}$

   (B) $\dfrac{b}{a}$

   (C) $a - b$

   (D) $a + b$

   (E) ab

10. If $3x$, $\dfrac{3}{x}$, and $\dfrac{15}{x}$ are integers, which of the following must also be an integer?

    I. $\dfrac{x}{3}$

    II. x

    III. $6x$

    (A) I only
    (B) II only
    (C) III only
    (D) I and III only
    (E) II and III only

Answers and Explanations: Problem Set 2

Easy

1. **E** Plug in 20 for x. If 10 people eat 20 quarts, and they all eat the same amount, then each person eats 2 quarts. Put a circle around 2. Go to the answers and remember that $x = 20$. (A) $= 10 \times 10 = 100$. Nope. (E) $= \dfrac{20}{10} = 2$. Yep.

2. **D** Plug in 2 for x and 2 for y. That satisfies the equation $\dfrac{x}{y} = 1$, and makes $x + y = 4$. Eliminate (B) and (C). How about $-2 = x$ and $-2 = y$? That makes $x + y = -4$. Eliminate (A) and (E).

3. **B** Plug in 5 for x, which makes $y = 3$. So $\dfrac{y}{3} = \dfrac{3}{3} = 1$. Circle 1. On to the answers, and plug in $x = 5$. (A) $= 5 - 3 = 2$. No good. (B) $= 5 - 4 = 1$. There you go.

Why do we keep saying "circle it" in the explanations? Because that's the arithmetic answer to the question. All that's left to do is plug in for the variables in the answer choices, and look for your circled number. We tell you to circle that number so it won't get lost in the shuffle, and you can keep track of what you're doing.

Notice how sometimes, as in question 2, you may have to plug in more than one set of numbers. That doesn't mean you're doing anything wrong, it's just the nature of the question—and it tends to happen on *must be* questions.

Also remember that you are trying to find numbers to plug in that make getting an answer to the question easy—so in question 3, if we'd plugged in $x = 2$, that would've made y negative. Who wants to deal with negatives if they don't have to? If some kind of nastiness happens, bail out and *pick new numbers*.

Medium

4. **D** Let $x = 7$ so $z = 1$. Try the answers. (D) is $6 + z$, or $6 + 1 = 7$. No sweat.

5. **D** Plug in 10 for x, which makes $y = 20$. Remember that a triangle has $180°$, so the third angle, z, must equal $180 - 30 = 150$. Circle 150. Try the answers, with $x = 10$. (D) gives us $180 - 30 = 150$.

6. **D** First put the inequalities in order: $w > x > y > z$. Plug in consecutive positive numbers for the variables: $w = 5$, $x = 4$, $y = 3$, $z = 2$. Now try the answers.

> (A) $4 + 2 = 5$. No, so leave it in.
>
> (B) $3 + 2 = 4$. No, so leave it in.
>
> (C) $4 - 3 = 2$. No, so leave it in.
>
> (D) $5 - 4 = 3$. No, so leave it in.
>
> (E) $5 - 2 = 3$. Yes, so cross it out.

Try a new set of numbers. $w = 4$, $x = 3$, $y = 2$, and $z = 1$. This time (A), (B), and (C) all work, so get rid of them—that leaves (D) as our answer. Watch out when the question says CANNOT; it's all too easy to get mixed up and start thinking in the wrong direction. Look for answers that *work* and cross them out, rather than looking for the answer that *doesn't* work.

7. **C** First, draw yourself a picture. (Think shoebox.) Plug in 2 for x. The formula for volume of a rectangular solid is length × width × height—in this case, xyz. Our volume is $12x = 12(2) = 24$. Let's come up with 3 different numbers—2 is one of them—that give us 24 when multiplied together.

A chart is never a bad idea. It keeps you organized.

x	y	z
2	1	12

Since y is as low as possible, z is as big as possible. Go with it. If you're not convinced, try other combinations—but don't forget, the question asks for the greatest possible value of z.

HARD

8. **B** Since there are a lot of exponents, plug in the smallest numbers you can. Positive/negative is what this question is about. Let's take it part by part. If $x^3 < 0$, you know x must be negative: Let $x = -1$. If $-1(y^2z)$ is positive, let $z = -2$. Beware! You don't know whether y is positive or negative, so you can't plug in anything for it. Look at I, II, and III, and remember you're looking for something that *must be* true:

   I. $xyz = -1(y)(-2)$. Maybe it's positive and maybe it isn't. It depends on the sign of y, and you don't know the sign of y.

   II. $x^2y^2z = 1(y^2)(-2)$. Sorry. It's negative.

   III. $x^3y^2z^3 = -1(y^2)(-2^3)$. Well, well, well. Since y is squared, it has to be positive. And the product of the other two negatives equals positive. It works.

9. **D** Plug in 11 for a and 5 for b. Those two choices satisfy all the conditions of the problem. Check the answers: (A) and (B) are fractions, forget about 'em. (C) is $11 - 5 = 6$, which isn't divisible by 8. (D) gives you $11 + 5 = 16$. If you divide 16 by 8, you get a quotient of 2 and a remainder of 0. End of story.

10. **C** How about plugging in 3 for x? Try the answers—you're looking for integers, so if the answer isn't an integer, you can cross it out.

   I. $\dfrac{x}{3} = \dfrac{3}{3} = 1$ OK so far.

   II. $x = 3$ OK so far.

   III. $6x = 6 \cdot 3 = 18$.   OK so far.

   At this point, your average test taker figures the question is pretty easy and picks (E). Not you, my friend. *This is a hard question.* You must go an extra step. Plug in a new number. Since the question concerns integers, what if you plug in something that isn't an integer? Like $x = \dfrac{1}{3}$?

   I. $\dfrac{\frac{1}{3}}{3} = \dfrac{1}{9}$. That's no integer. Cross it out.

   II. $\dfrac{1}{3}$. No good either.

   III. $6\left(\dfrac{1}{3}\right) = 2$. Okay.

   Since you have eliminated I and II, only III remains.

PROBLEM SET 3: PLUGGING IN THE ANSWER CHOICES

EASY

1. If x is a positive integer, and $x + 12 = x^2$, what is the value of x ?

   (A) 2
   (B) 4
   (C) 6
   (D) 8
   (E) 12

2. If twice the sum of three consecutive numbers is 12, and the two lowest numbers add up to 3, what is the highest number?

   (A) 2
   (B) 3
   (C) 6
   (D) 9
   (E) 12

3. If $2^x = 8^{(x-4)}$, then $x =$

   (A) 4
   (B) 6
   (C) 8
   (D) 9
   (E) 64

MEDIUM

4. If Jane bought 3 equally priced shirts on sale, she would have 2 dollars left over. If instead she bought 10 equally priced pairs of socks, she would have 7 dollars left over. If the prices of both shirts and socks are integers, which of the following, in dollars, could be the amount that Jane has to spend?

   (A) 28
   (B) 32
   (C) 47
   (D) 57
   (E) 60

5. During a vacation together, Bob spent twice as much as Josh, who spent four times as much as Ralph. If Bob and Ralph together spent $180, how much did Josh spend?

(A) $20
(B) $80
(C) $120
(D) $160
(E) $180

6. Tina has half as many marbles as Louise. If Louise gave away 3 of her marbles and lost 2 more, she would have 1 more marble than Tina. How many marbles does Tina have?

(A) 2
(B) 3
(C) 5
(D) 6
(E) 7

7. In a bag of jellybeans, $\frac{1}{3}$ are cherry and $\frac{1}{4}$ are licorice. If the remaining 20 jellybeans are orange, how many jellybeans are in the bag?

(A) 12
(B) 16
(C) 32
(D) 36
(E) 48

HARD

8. If the circumference of a circle is equal to twice its area, then the area of the circle equals

(A) 2
(B) π
(C) 2π
(D) 4π
(E) 16π

9. If $r = \dfrac{6}{3s + 2}$ and $tr = \dfrac{2}{3s + 2}$, then $t =$

(A) $\dfrac{1}{4}$

(B) $\dfrac{1}{3}$

(C) 2

(D) 3

(E) 4

10. If x^2 is added to $\dfrac{5}{4y}$, the sum is $\dfrac{5+y}{4y}$. If y is a positive integer, which of the following is the value of x ?

(A) $\dfrac{1}{4}$

(B) $\dfrac{1}{2}$

(C) $\dfrac{4}{5}$

(D) 1

(E) 5

Answers and Explanations: Problem Set 3

Easy

1. **B** Start with (C), 6 = x. That gives you 6 + 12 = 36. No good. At this point, don't stare at the other choices, waiting for divine inspiration—just pick another one and try it. It's okay if the next answer you try isn't right either. If you plug in 4 for x, you get 4 + 12 = 16. The equation works, so that's that.

2. **B** Start with (C). If the highest number is 6, the other two are 5 and 4. 5 and 4 don't add up to 3—cross out (C). Try (B). If the highest number is 3, the other two numbers are 1 and 2. (They have to be consecutive.) The sum of 3 + 2 + 1= 6, and twice the sum of 6 = 12. If you picked (A), you didn't pay attention to what the question asked for. Be sure to reread the question so you know which number they want.

3. **B** Try (C) first. Does $2^8 = 8^4$? Nope. (Use your calculator.) Try something lower, like (B). Does $2^6 = 8^2$? Yes.

Medium

4. **C** Try (C) first. If Jane has $47 to spend, 47 ÷ 3 = 15 with 2 left over. (The shirts cost $15 apiece.) Now try 47 ÷ 10 = 4, with 7 left over. (Socks are $4 a pair.) It works.

5. **B** Try (C) first. If Josh spent $120, Bob spent $240 and Ralph spent $40. That means Bob and Ralph together spent $280, not $180 as the problem tells us. (C) is no good. Since your number is way too big, try something smaller. If Josh spent $80, Bob spent $160 and Ralph spent $20. So Bob and Ralph together spent $180. That's more like it.

6. **D** Start with (C). If Tina has 5 marbles, then Louise has 10. If Louise gives away 3, then she has 7. If she loses 2 more, she's down to 5. You're supposed to end up with Louise having 1 more than Tina, but they both have 5. Cross out (C)—and you know you're close to the right answer. Try (D) If Tina has 6, Louise has 12. If Louise gives away and loses 5, she's got 7, which is 1 more than Tina has.

7. **E** Try (C) first. Oops—$\frac{1}{3}$ of 32 is a fraction. Forget (C). Try (D): $\frac{1}{3}$ of 36 = 12. $\frac{1}{4}$ of 36 = 9. Does 12 + 9 + 20 = 36? No. Try (E). $\frac{1}{3}$ of 48 = 16. $\frac{1}{4}$ of 48 = 12. Does 16 + 12 + 20 = 48? Yes!

Making a simple chart will help you keep track of your work:

	D	E
cherry	12	16
licorice	9	12
orange	20	20
TOTAL	41	48

HARD

8. **B** Try (C) first. If the area is 2π, then the radius becomes a fraction. That's probably not going to be the answer, so you should move on. Try (B). If the area is π, then the radius is 1. ($\pi r^2 = \pi$, $r^2 = 1$, $r = 1$.) If $r = 1$, the circumference is $2\pi(1) = 2\pi$. So the circumference is twice the area. Beautiful.

9. **B** Try (C) first. If $t = 2$, then look at the second equation:

$$2r = \frac{2}{3s+2}$$

$$r = \frac{2}{3s+2} \bullet \frac{1}{2}$$

$$r = \frac{1}{3s+2}$$

Compare that to the first equation. No good. Try (B). If $t = \frac{1}{3}$, then

$$\frac{r}{3} = 2(3s+2)$$

$$r = \frac{2}{3s+2} \bullet 3$$

$$r = \frac{6}{3s+2}$$

Same as the first equation. You're done.

10. **B** Choice (C) is particularly nasty here, so ignore it. Try Choice (D), plugging in 1 for x. You get $1 + \dfrac{5}{4y} = \dfrac{4y+5}{4y}$ or $1 = \dfrac{1}{4}$. (The y drops out.) (B) gives you $\dfrac{1}{4} + \dfrac{5}{4y} = \dfrac{5+y}{4y}$ or $\dfrac{1}{4} = \dfrac{1}{4}$. You could also solve by plugging in—choose a positive integer for y, plug it into the equation, and see what happens. You end up with $x = \dfrac{1}{2}$.

> When you're plugging in, start with (C) unless (C) is hard to work with, as in question 10. In that case, try the integers, since they'll be easier to do anyway. And don't worry if you have to try a couple of answer choices before you hit the right one—the first one you do is always the slowest, because you're still finding your way. Subsequent tries should be easier. And plugging in is always easier than writing equations.

PROBLEM SET 4: MORE PLUGGING IN THE ANSWER CHOICES

EASY

1. If $\dfrac{a-4}{28} = \dfrac{1}{4}$, then $a =$

   (A) 11

   (B) 10

   (C) 7

   (D) 6

   (E) $\dfrac{3}{28}$

2. If the area of $\triangle ABC$ is 21, and the length of the height minus the length of the base equals 1, then the base of the triangle is equal to

   (A) 1
   (B) 2
   (C) 4
   (D) 6
   (E) 7

3. If $d^2 = \sqrt{4} + d + 10$, then $d =$

   (A) –2
   (B) 2
   (C) 3
   (D) 4
   (E) 16

MEDIUM

4. If $\dfrac{4}{x-1} = \dfrac{x+1}{2}$, which of the following is a possible value of x ?

   (A) –1
   (B) 0
   (C) 1
   (D) 2
   (E) 3

5. The product of the digits of a two-digit number is 6. If the tens digit is subtracted from the units digit, the result is 5. What is the two-digit number?

    (A) 61
    (B) 32
    (C) 27
    (D) 23
    (E) 16

6. If $16{,}000 = 400(x + 9)$, what is the value of x?

    (A) 391
    (B) 310
    (C) 40
    (D) 31
    (E) 4

7. What is the radius of a circle with an area of $\frac{\pi}{4}$?

    (A) 0.2
    (B) 0.4
    (C) 0.5
    (D) 2
    (E) 4

HARD

8. If 20 percent of x is 36 less than x percent of $x - 70$, what is the value of x?

    (A) 140
    (B) 120
    (C) 110
    (D) 100
    (E) 50

9. If $x^2 = y^3$ and $(x - y)^2 = 2x$, then y could equal

    (A) 64
    (B) 16
    (C) 8
    (D) 4
    (E) 2

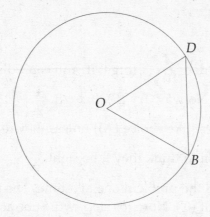

10. In the figure above, $OD = DB$ and arc $DB = 2\pi$. What is the area of the circle?

(A) 64π
(B) 36π
(C) 16π
(D) 12π
(E) 4π

Answers and Explanations: Problem Set 4

Easy

1. **A** Try (C) first. Does $\dfrac{3}{28} = \dfrac{1}{4}$? Nope. Look for a bigger number—(B) gives you $\dfrac{6}{28}$, which is closer, but still no cigar. (A) gives you $\dfrac{7}{28} = \dfrac{1}{4}$.

2. **D** Try (C) first. If the base = 4, then $h - 4 = 1$ and $h = 5$. The formula for area of a triangle is $\dfrac{1}{2}bh$, so the area would be 10. Too small. Try (D). If the base is 6, then $h - 6 = 1$ and $h = 7$. The area is $\dfrac{42}{2} = 21$.

3. **D** Yes, it looks nasty, but it's a breeze with the miracle of plugging in the answer choices. As always, try (C) first: $3^2 = \sqrt{4} + 3 + 10$; $9 = 2 + 13$. Forget it. Try (D). $4^2 = 2 + 4 + 10$; $16 = 16$. That's it.

> If you try (C) and it doesn't work, take a second to see if you need a higher or lower number. But if you can't tell *quickly*, don't spend too much time thinking about it—just try (B) or (D) and keep going.

4. **E** Try (C) first. If $x = 1$, does $\dfrac{4}{0}$ . . . forget it. You can't divide by 0. Try (D). If $x = 2$, does $\dfrac{4}{1} = \dfrac{3}{2}$? No way. Try (E). If $x = 3$, $\dfrac{4}{2} = \dfrac{4}{2}$. Yes. Remember to avoid trying negatives [like choice (A)] unless they're all you have left or you have some reason to think they'll be right.

5. **E** Take the directions of the problem one at a time. The product of the digits = 6, so cross out (C). Now for step two. Subtract the tens digit from the units digit, and look for 5. (E) does it. If you picked (A), you subtracted the units digit from the tens digit, which means you don't know the definitions (see the definitions review at the beginning of the Arithmetic section) or you didn't reread the question to see what your next direction was. Always reread the question before continuing on to the next step.

6. **D** Try (C) first. Does $400 \cdot 49 = 16{,}000$? No, and hopefully you just estimate that and don't bother doing it, with or without your calculator. How about (D)? $400(40) = 16{,}000$. Yep. If you picked (A), you miscounted the zeros. Try checking your answers on your calculator.

7. **C** Fabulous plugging in question. Try (C) first. Convert 0.5 to a fraction, because fractions are better than decimals and because the question has a fraction in it. If the radius is $\dfrac{1}{2}$, the area is $\pi\left(\dfrac{1}{2}\right)^2 = \pi\left(\dfrac{1}{4}\right) = \dfrac{\pi}{4}$.

> **Why do we like fractions better than decimals?**
>
> Mostly because that irritating little decimal point is so easily misplaced. Also because decimals can get very tiny and hard to estimate. You don't want to convert decimals to fractions automatically—only when the question would be easier to do that way. If the question is in decimals and the answers are in decimals, then don't bother converting.

HARD

8. **B** Try (D) first because the question is about percents and 100 is easy to do. 20% of 100 is 20. 100% of 100 – 70 is 30. Does 30 – 20 = 46? Nah. Try (B). 20% of 120 is 24. 120% of 50 is 60. Does 60 – 24 = 36? Yes.

9. **D** Try (C) first. If $y = 8$, then $x^2 = 8^3$. $8^3 = 512$. If $x^2 = 512$, x isn't an integer. Forget (C). Try (D). If $y = 4$, then $x^2 = 4^3$. $x^2 = 64$; $x = 8$. Now try them in the second equation: $(8 – 4)^2 = 2(8)$. $4^2 = 16$. It works. Notice that when (C) didn't work, you went with a smaller number because it was easier.

10. **B** First, write in 2π beside arc DB. Now try (C). If the area is 16π, the radius is 4. Write in 4 beside the two radii, and also DB, because $OD = DB$. Aha! That makes triangle DOB equilateral! Since angle DOB is 60°, and $\frac{60}{360} = \frac{1}{6}$, that makes arc DB $\frac{1}{6}$ of the circumference. Remember our radius is 4, so the circumference is 8π. Uh oh— 2π is not $\frac{1}{6}$ of 8π. So cross off (C). But at least now you know what to do. Try (B). If the area is 36π, the radius is 6 and the circumference is 12π. $\frac{1}{6}$ of 12π is 2π. Yeah! Did that seem really painful? It was a lot of work, but then, it was a hard question. The reason plugging in is a good technique for this problem is that if you plug in the answer choices, you get to move through the question like a robot, one step after the other, and you don't have to depend on a flash of insight.

PROBLEM SET 5: ESTIMATING

EASY

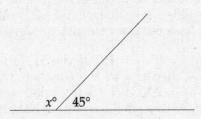

1. What is the value of 2x ?

    (A) 360
    (B) 270
    (C) 135
    (D) 90
    (E) 67.5

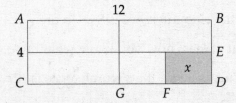

2. If F is equidistant from G and D, and E is equidistant from B and D, what fractional part of rectangle ABDC is area x ?

    (A) $\frac{1}{16}$

    (B) $\frac{1}{8}$

    (C) $\frac{1}{4}$

    (D) $\frac{1}{3}$

    (E) $\frac{1}{2}$

3. If Sarah bought 12 pies for $30, how many pies could she have bought for $37.50 at the same rate?

(A) 3
(B) 9
(C) 12
(D) 15
(E) 21

Medium

4. If a runner completes one lap of a track in 64 seconds, approximately how many minutes will it take her to run 40 laps at the same speed?

(A) 25
(B) 30
(C) 43
(D) 52
(E) 128

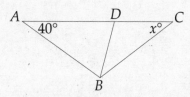

5. In the figure above, $BD = DC$ and $AB = AD$. What is the value of x ?

(A) 110
(B) 70
(C) 55
(D) 35
(E) 15

6. Martina wants to buy as many felt-tip pens as possible for $10. If the pens cost between $1.75 and $2.30, what is the greatest number of pens Martina can buy?

(A) 4
(B) 5
(C) 6
(D) 7
(E) 8

7. 1.2 is what percent of 600 ?

(A) 0.002%
(B) 0.2%
(C) 5%
(D) 20%
(E) 500%

Hard

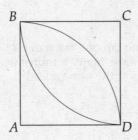

8. In the figure above, *ABCD* is a square with sides of 4. What is the length of arc *BD* ?

(A) 8π
(B) 4π
(C) 3π
(D) 2π
(E) π

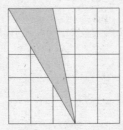

9. Each of the small squares in the figure above has an area of 4. If the shortest side of the triangle is equal in length to 2 sides of a small square, what is the area of the shaded triangle?

(A) 160
(B) 40
(C) 24
(D) 20
(E) 16

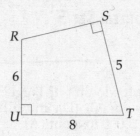

Note: Figure not drawn to scale.

10. In the figure above, what is the length of *RS* ?

(A) 10

(B) $5\sqrt{3}$

(C) 8

(D) $\sqrt{5}$

(E) $2\sqrt{3}$

ANSWERS AND EXPLANATIONS: PROBLEM SET 5

EASY

1. **B** Estimate first: x looks pretty big, doesn't it? Bigger than 90? Yes. So $2x$ will be bigger than 180. Cross out (C), (D), and (E). Is x a line of 180? Of course not. So $2x$ is less than 360. Cross out (A).

2. **B** Use your eyeballs and compare against the answer choices. Does x look like $\frac{1}{2}$ of the rectangle? No? Cross out (E). What about $\frac{1}{3}$? Cross out (D). $\frac{1}{4}$? Cross out (C). Could you fit 16 xs in the rectangle? No—cross out (A). It's also helpful to draw more boxes in the figure, and then you could count them up:

3. **E** $37.50 is going to buy more pies than $30, right? So cross out anything less than or equal to 12. Say goodbye to (A), (B), and (C). Now, any chance an extra 7.50 will buy nearly another 12 pies? No. Eliminate (E).

MEDIUM

4. **C** This is a great question for estimating. Don't like 64 seconds? Call it 60, or 1 minute. If the runner completes a lap in just over a minute, she'll complete 40 laps in just over 40 minutes. Only (C) is close.

5. **D** First just eyeball the angle. It's smaller than 90°. It's close to angle BAD, which is marked 40. You're down to (C) and (D). Is it a little smaller than BAD or 15° bigger than BAD? Go for it! You can always come back and check your answer the long way if you have time.

   The long way: BAD is isosceles, since $AB = AD$. The two base angles of $BAD = 140$, so each is 70°. If $\angle BDA = 70°$, then $\angle BDC$ is 110°. Triangle BDC is isosceles too, with $\angle DCB$ and $\angle CBD = x°$. $2x = 70$, so $x = 35°$. Now admit it—isn't estimating easier?

6. **B** If Martina wants to buy as many pens as possible, she wants to buy the cheapest ones she can. Try plugging in the answer choices. Start with (C). If she buys 6 for $1.75, that equals $10.50. A bit more than $10, so pick the next lowest answer choice.

7. **B** 600 is pretty big, and 1.2 is pretty tiny. So you should be looking for a pretty small percentage. Cross out (D) and (E), and maybe even (C). Then use your calculator. The easiest way to figure out your next step would be to set up a proportion:

$$\frac{1.2}{600} = \frac{x}{100}$$

Or transform the sentence:

$$1.2 = \frac{x}{100} \bullet 600$$

Only 0.2, (B), fits the proportion.

HARD

8. **D** First mark the sides of the square with 4. Now estimate the length of *BD*, based on the side of the square. Think of the side of the square as a piece of spaghetti that you are going to drape over *BD*. So *BD* is longer than 4. Maybe around 6? Now go to the answers, and substitute 3 for π. (You know, $\pi = 3.14$, but you don't have to be so exact. You're just estimating.) Choice (A) is around 24. Way too big. (B) is around 12, (C) is around 9, and (D) is around 6. (E) is too small. Pick (D) and move on.

9. **D** When you estimate, remember that each shaded square has an area of 4. It's tricky to do this exactly, because mostly only slivers of squares are shaded. So fake it. Almost 2 full squares at the top, another square on the next row (that's 3 so far) and then slivers on the next 3 rows that make up about 2 full squares. So you've got 5 squares each with area 4; the area of the triangle is around 20, so pick (D).

   So you want to cross out (A) and (B) and then get the answer exactly? You can do that. If each square has an area of 4, then the side of a little square is 2. Write that on the figure, in a couple of places. Now use the top of the triangle as the base. It equals 4. The other thing you need is the height, or altitude, of the triangle—and in this case, the height is equal to a side of the big square, or 10. Using the formula for the area of a triangle, plug 4 in for the base and 10 in for the height and you get 20 for the area.

10. **B** Hey, wake up! You can't estimate anything if the figure isn't drawn to scale! But you may want to re-draw the figure to make it look more like it's supposed to look. Now for the solution: Draw a line from *R* to *T*, slicing the figure into 2 triangles. Now all you have to do is use the Pythagorean theorem to calculate the lengths. Triangle *RUT* is a 6:8:10 triangle, a Pythagorean triple. Now for *RST*: $a^2 + 5^2 = 10^2$. So $a^2 = 75$ and $a = 5\sqrt{3}$.

PROBLEM SET 6: FACTORS, MULTIPLES, AND PRIMES

EASY

1. If t is even, which of the following expressions must be odd?

   (A) $t - 2$

   (B) t^2

   (C) $2(t + 1)$

   (D) $t(t + 1)$

   (E) $t + 3$

2. If m is a multiple of 5, and n is a factor of 3, which of the following could equal 13 ?

   (A) mn

   (B) $m + n$

   (C) $\dfrac{m}{n}$

   (D) $\dfrac{n}{m}$

   (E) $m - n$

Set A: {0, 1, 2, 3, 4, 5}
Set B: {1, 2, 7, 9, 10}

3. How many members of Set A are factors of any member of Set B ?

   (A) 2
   (B) 3
   (C) 4
   (D) 5
   (E) 6

MEDIUM

4. Which of the following equations is equal to
   $6y + 6x = 66$?

   (A) $33 = x + y$
   (B) $33 = 2y + 2x$
   (C) $11 - x = y$
   (D) $11 - 2x = y$
   (E) $4y - 4x = 44$

5. If the greatest prime factor of 32 is a, and the
   least prime factor of 77 is b, then ab is divisible
   by which of the following numbers?

   (A) 3
   (B) 4
   (C) 8
   (D) 11
   (E) 14

6. If $[x]$ is defined as the greatest prime factor of x
   minus the least prime factor of x, then what is
   the value of $\dfrac{[20]}{[10]}$?

   (A) 10

   (B) 5

   (C) 2

   (D) 1

   (E) $\dfrac{1}{2}$

7. If p is the number of prime numbers between 65
   and 75, then $p =$

   (A) 0
   (B) 1
   (C) 2
   (D) 3
   (E) 4

8. If r, s, and t are positive integers, and $rs = t$, then which of the following must be true?

   I. $r < t$
   II. $r \leq t$
   III. $s \geq t$

   (A) I only
   (B) II only
   (C) III only
   (D) I and III only
   (E) II and III only

9. If $12y = x^3$, and x and y are positive integers, what is the least possible value for y ?

   (A) 3
   (B) 9
   (C) 18
   (D) 27
   (E) 64

10. The alarm of Clock A rings every 4 minutes, the alarm of Clock B rings every 6 minutes, and the alarm of Clock C rings every 7 minutes. If the alarms of all three clocks ring at 12:00 noon, the next time at which all the alarms will ring at exactly the same time is

   (A) 12:28 P.M.
   (B) 12:56 P.M.
   (C)   1:24 P.M.
   (D)   1:36 P.M.
   (E)   2:48 P.M.

ANSWERS AND EXPLANATIONS: PROBLEM SET 6

EASY

1. **E** Plug in an even number for t. How about $t = 2$? Now go to the answers, looking for something to be odd. (A) 0, (B) 4, (C) 6, (D) 10, and (E) 5. And remember that anything multiplied by an even number will be even, so you can eliminate (B), (C), and (D).

2. **B** Plug in again. Make $m = 10$ and $n = 3$. Run those through the answer choices, looking for 13. Choice (B) is $m + n$, or $10 + 3$ or 13. If you picked other numbers and didn't get an answer, don't get frustrated or think you're doing something wrong. Just pick another set of numbers, and make sure your numbers fit the directions of the problem (i.e., the number you pick for m has to be a multiple of 5, and the number you pick for n has to be either 1 or 3).

3. **C** Be methodical about this. Take each number in Set *A*, one at a time, and see if it divides evenly into anything in Set *B*. 0 isn't a factor of anything but 0. 1 is a factor of everything in Set *B*. Put a check by 1. 2 is a factor of 2, so put a check by 2. 3 is a factor of 9, so put a check by 3. 4 isn't a factor of anything in Set *B*. 5 is a factor of 10, so put a check by 5. How many checks do you have? Four of them.

MEDIUM

4. **C** Try reducing the equation in the question first, by dividing the whole thing by 6. That leaves you with $x + y = 11$. That's the same as (C), if you just move the x to the other side.

5. **E** There's only one prime factor of 32, and it's 2. The prime factors of 77 are 7 and 11, so the smallest is 7. That makes $ab = 14$, which is certainly divisible by 14.

6. **D** This is a function question, as we're sure you noticed. First deal with [20]. The greatest prime factor of 20 is 5, and the least prime factor is 2. $5 - 2 = 3$, so [20] = 3. Now for [10]. The greatest prime factor of 10 is 5, and the least prime factor is 2. So [10] = $5 - 2 = 3$. $\frac{3}{3} = 1$.

7. **D** First write out the numbers: 66, 67, 68, 69, 70, 71, 72, 73, 74. Be methodical—cross out anything that's even: 66, 68, 70, 72, 74. Now cross out anything left that's divisible by 3: 69. Any number divisible by 4, 6, or 8 is even, and you've already crossed those out. Any number divisible by 9 is also divisible by 3, and you've crossed that out. All you have left is 7—you're left with 67, 71, and 73. None of them is divisible by 7, so they're all prime.

HARD

8. **B** Plug in. Make a chart:

r	s	t
1	2	2
1	1	1
2	3	6

That should do it. Now check our numbers against I, II, and III. I isn't true if r, s, and t all equal 1. III isn't true if $r = 2$, $s = 3$, and $t = 6$. That leaves you with II.

Why bother with a chart? On *must be* questions, picking one set of numbers probably isn't going to be enough. This question is pretty tricky for a medium, because I is true except when all the variables equal 1. But then I and II only isn't a choice, so you have to disprove one of them.

9. **C** Solve this problem with a combination of factoring and plugging in. The question looks like this: $2 \times 2 \times 3y = x^3$. Now factor the answer choices. Choice (A) is $3 \bullet 1$. If you plug that in for y, does it give you a cube? Nope. (B) is $3 \bullet 3$. No good either. (C) is $2 \times 3 \times 3$—now you have (2×3) $(2 \times 3)(2 \times 3) = x^3$. It works.

Another way to do this problem is more straightforward plugging in: Plug in the answers for y, and use your calculator to see if that product is a cube root. If your calculator doesn't have the x^y function, then make a list of cubes to see if the product is on it.

10. **C** Ouch—this one is ugly. You can't simply multiply $4 \times 6 \times 7$ and add 168 minutes to 12:00. You'll get (E), and while it's true that all 3 alarms would ring at 2:48, that's not the *earliest* time they would ring at the same time. (And that solution is too easy for a hard question.) Instead, factor the ringing rates, so you get (2×2), (2×3), and (7). The lowest common multiple will be $2 \times 2 \times 3 \times 7$. Four goes in evenly, and so do 6 and 7. Now multiply it, and you get 84, which is 1 hour and 24 minutes. Add that to 12:00, and you're done.

> When you're plugging in the answer choices, remember that if the question asks for the *least possible value*, start with the smallest answer choice. For *greatest possible value*, start with the biggest answer choice. That way you won't get caught picking an answer that works, but isn't the *least* or *greatest* answer that works.

PROBLEM SET 7: FRACTIONS, DECIMALS, AND PERCENTS

EASY

1. A big-screen TV is on sale at 15% off the regular price. If the regular price of the TV is $420, what is the sale price?

    (A) $63
    (B) $126
    (C) $357
    (D) $405
    (E) $435

2. Which of the following is the decimal form of
    $$70 + \frac{7}{10} + \frac{3}{1000}?$$

    (A) 70.0703
    (B) 70.7003
    (C) 70.703
    (D) 70.73
    (E) 77.003

3. Six more than two-thirds of twelve is

    (A) 10
    (B) 12
    (C) 14
    (D) 18
    (E) 22

MEDIUM

4. Walking at a constant rate, Stuart takes 24 minutes to walk to the nearest bus stop, and $\frac{1}{3}$ of that time to walk to the movie theater. It takes him half the time to walk to school than it does for him to walk to the movie theater. How many minutes does it take Stuart to walk to school?

   (A) 36
   (B) 24
   (C) 16
   (D) 8
   (E) 4

5. What is the value of x if $\dfrac{\frac{1}{2}}{x} = 4$?

   (A) 8

   (B) 2

   (C) $\dfrac{1}{2}$

   (D) $\dfrac{1}{4}$

   (E) $\dfrac{1}{8}$

6. If $x\%$ of y is 10, then $y\%$ of x is

   (A) 1
   (B) 5
   (C) 10
   (D) 50
   (E) 90

7. A certain drink is made by adding 4 parts water to 1 part drink mix. If the amount of water is doubled, and the amount of drink mix is quadrupled, what percent of the new mixture is drink mix?

(A) 30%

(B) $33\frac{1}{3}\%$

(C) 50%

(D) $66\frac{2}{3}\%$

(E) 80%

Hard

8. Set A consists of distinct fractions, each of which has a numerator of 1 and a denominator d such that $1 < d < 8$, where d is an integer. If Set B consists of the reciprocals of the fractions with odd denominators in Set A, then the product of Set A and Set B =

(A) $\frac{1}{96}$

(B) $\frac{1}{48}$

(C) $\frac{1}{24}$

(D) 1

(E) 8

9. For all values x, if x is even, x^* is defined as $0.5x$; if x is odd, x^* is defined as $\frac{x}{3}$. What is the value of $\frac{(6a)^*}{9^*}$?

(A) $2a$
(B) $3a$
(C) a^*
(D) $(2a)^*$
(E) $(4a)^*$

10. If a, b, and c are distinct positive integers, and
10% of abc is 5, then $a + b$ could equal

  (A) 1
  (B) 3
  (C) 5
  (D) 8
  (E) 25

ANSWERS AND EXPLANATIONS: PROBLEM SET 7

EASY

1. **C** The numbers are too awkward to plug in, so do it the old-fashioned way: 15% of $420 is $0.15 \times 420 = 63$. $420 - 63 = 357$. Use your calculator.

2. **C** Take the pieces one at a time and eliminate. The first piece is 70: eliminate (E). The second piece is $\frac{7}{10}$, or 0.7. Eliminate (A). The last piece is $\frac{3}{1000}$, or 0.003. Eliminate (B) and (D). If you want to do the conversions on your calculator, that's cool. But adding the fractions together and then converting to a decimal would take more time, calculator or no calculator.

3. **C** Translate the problem into math language: $6 + \frac{2}{3} \times 12 = ?$. Then, don't forget PEMDAS: Multiply before you add. $6 + \frac{2}{3}(12) = 6 + 8 = 14$.

MEDIUM

4. **E** Start working from the 24 minutes it takes poor Stuart to walk to the bus stop. (Won't anybody give the guy a ride?) If it takes $\frac{1}{3}$ of 24 to walk to the movies, that's 8 minutes. If it takes him half of that time to walk to school, $\frac{1}{2}$ of 8 is 4. This question requires close reading more than anything else.

5. **E** Plugging in the answer choices wouldn't be a bad idea here—you can eliminate (A) and (B) pretty quickly that way. (C) gives you $\dfrac{\frac{1}{2}}{\frac{1}{2}} = 1$. (D) is $\dfrac{\frac{1}{2}}{\frac{1}{4}} = 2$. (E) is $\dfrac{\frac{1}{2}}{\frac{1}{8}} = 4$.

6. **C** Plug in 10 for y, which makes $x = 100$. Plug those numbers into the second part: 100% of 10 = 10.

7. **B** First make a little chart: If you double the water and quadruple the mix, you get

water		mix
4	:	1
8	:	4

Reread the question. It asks for the percentage of the new mixture that's drink mix. You've got $\dfrac{4\,(\text{mix})}{12\,(\text{total})}$, which equals $\dfrac{1}{3}$, or $33\dfrac{1}{3}\%$.

If you made it almost to the end but picked (C), don't forget that you have to express the mix as a percentage of the total, not a percentage of the water.

HARD

8. **B** Read this carefully. Set A has different fractions, each with a numerator of 1. (You might as well write them down like that and fill in the denominators when you get there.) The denominators are between 1 and 8. That gives you Set A: $\dfrac{1}{2}, \dfrac{1}{3}, \dfrac{1}{4}, \dfrac{1}{5}, \dfrac{1}{6}, \dfrac{1}{7}$. Set B has the reciprocals of the members of Set A with odd denominators, so Set B: $\dfrac{3}{1}, \dfrac{5}{1}, \dfrac{7}{1}$. Now multiply the sets together—see how the fractions that have reciprocals cancel each other out? You're left with $\dfrac{1}{2} \times \dfrac{1}{4} \times \dfrac{1}{6}$, which is $\dfrac{1}{48}$.

9. **D** It's a function, so just follow the directions. Looking at the numerator, $6a$ has to be even because it has an even number as a factor. (Or plug in any low number for a.) Since $6a$ is even, follow the first direction: $6a \times 0.5 = 3a$. Now for the denominator: 9 is odd, so follow the second direction. $\dfrac{9}{3} = 3$. So $\dfrac{(6a)^*}{9^*} = \dfrac{3a}{3} = a$. Did you pick (C)? Well, sorry, you aren't getting off that easy. (C), (D), and (E) are functions, too, so you have to translate them, looking for your answer, a. Skip (A) and (B). For (D), $(2a)$ is even, so $(2a)^* = 2a \times 0.5 = a$.

10. **B** First translate the middle part of the problem into an equation. 10% of abc is 5 translates to $\dfrac{10}{100} \bullet abc = 5$. Now solve for abc, and you get $abc = 50$. Reread the question. Each variable is different, each is positive, and multiplied together they produce 50. Now plug in the answer choices, and remember that the answers represent $a + b$. Choice (A) is silly, because it would make a and b fractions, and they can't be fractions. In (B), $a + b$ would have to be $1 + 2$. If $a = 1$ and $b = 2$ and $abc = 50$, what is c? $c = 25$, so it works.

A couple of reminders: If you are making mistakes on the easy and medium problems, don't spend a lot of time—if any—working on the hard problems. You need to hone your skills first; you may want to go back to the review section and do some work before continuing. And don't forget, you probably want to leave some questions blank on the real thing.

Speaking of leaving questions blank, question 9 would be a fine choice to avoid entirely. Long functions in the hard problems can be really nasty.

PROBLEM SET 8: AVERAGES, RATIOS, PROPORTIONS, AND PROBABILITIES

EASY

1. Three consecutive integers add up to 258. What is the smallest integer?

    (A) 58
    (B) 85
    (C) 86
    (D) 89
    (E) 94

2. A factory produces 6,000 plates per day. If one out of 15 plates is broken, how many unbroken plates does the factory produce each day?

    (A) 5800
    (B) 5600
    (C) 1500
    (D) 800
    (E) 400

3. It takes 4 friends 24 minutes to wash all the windows in Maria's house. The friends all work at the same rate. How long would it take 8 friends, working at the same rate, to wash all the windows in Maria's house?

    (A) 96
    (B) 32
    (C) 20
    (D) 12
    (E) 8

MEDIUM

4. The value of t is inversely proportional to the value of w. If value of w increases by a factor of 5, what happens to the value of t ?

    (A) t increases by a factor of 5.
    (B) t increases by a factor of 2.
    (C) t remains constant.
    (D) t decreases by a factor of 2.
    (E) t decreases by a factor of 5.

5. A drawer holds only blue socks and white socks. If the ratio of blue socks to white socks is 4:3, which of the following could be the total number of socks in the drawer?

(A) 4
(B) 7
(C) 8
(D) 12
(E) 24

6. The probability of choosing a caramel from a certain bag of candy is $\frac{1}{5}$, and the probability of choosing a butterscotch is $\frac{5}{8}$. If the bag contains 40 pieces of candy, and the only types of candy in the bag are caramel, butterscotch, and fudge, how many pieces of fudge are in the bag?

(A) 5
(B) 7
(C) 8
(D) 16
(E) 25

7. Dixie spent an average of x dollars on each of 5 shirts and an average of y dollars on each of 3 hats. In terms of x and y, how many dollars did she spend on shirts and hats?

(A) $5x + 3y$
(B) $3x + 5y$
(C) $15(x + y)$
(D) $8xy$
(E) $15xy$

HARD

8. The ratio of $\frac{1}{6} : \frac{1}{5}$ is equal to the ratio of 35 to

    (A) 24
    (B) 30
    (C) 36
    (D) 42
    (E) 45

9. An artist makes a certain shade of green paint by mixing blue and yellow in a ratio of 3:4. She makes orange by mixing red and yellow in a ratio of 2:3. If on one day she mixes both green and orange and uses equal amounts of blue and red paint, what fractional part of the paint that she uses is yellow?

    (A) $\dfrac{7}{12}$

    (B) $\dfrac{17}{29}$

    (C) $\dfrac{7}{5}$

    (D) $\dfrac{17}{12}$

    (E) $\dfrac{9}{6}$

10. The areas of two circles are in a ratio of 4:9. If both radii are integers, and $r_1 - r_2 = 2$, which of the following is the radius of the larger circle?

    (A) 4
    (B) 5
    (C) 6
    (D) 8
    (E) 9

Answers and Explanations: Problem Set 8

Easy

1. **B** If the three integers add up to 258, then their average is 258 ÷ 3, or 86. Since the integers are consecutive, they must be 85, 86, and 87. Check it on your calculator. If you picked (C), what did you do wrong? Forget what the question asked for? Divide 258 by 3 and then quit? Even easy problems may have more than one step. This would also be a good question to plug in the answer choices.

2. **B** First estimate. You're looking for the number of unbroken plates—if only one broke out of 15, there should be a lot of unbroken plates, right? Cross out (C), (D), and (E). Now set up a proportion:

$$\frac{\text{broken}}{\text{total}} = \frac{1}{15} = \frac{x}{6000}$$

And cross-multiply. You get $6000 = 15x$, so using your calculator, $x = 400$. That's the number of broken plates, so subtract 400 from 6000 and you've got the answer. If you picked (E), you could have gotten the problem right if you had either estimated first or reread the question right before you answered it.

3. **D** There are twice as many people, so the work will go twice as fast. You can't set up a normal proportion because it's an inverse proportion—the more people you have, the less time the work takes. So if you multiply the number of people by 2, you divide the work time by 2. Don't forget to use your common sense.

Medium

4. **E** Since no values were given, try plugging in values of your own to test what happens. If t starts out as 10 and w starts out as 5, you can set up the formula for inverse variation as follows: $t_1 w_1 = t_2 w_2$. In this case, the t_1 is 10, w_1 is 5, and w_2 is 25 (since you multiply it by 5). So set up the equation as: $10 \times 5 = t_2 \times 25$. $\frac{50}{25} t = 2$. So what happened to the value of t? It decreased by a factor of 5.

5. **B** The total must be the sum of the numbers in a ratio, or a multiple of that sum. In this case, $4 + 3 = 7$, so the number of socks could be 7 or any multiple of 7. (You can have fractions in a ratio, it's true, but not when you're dealing with socks or people or anything that you can't chop into pieces. And probably not on a medium question, either.)

6. **B** Here's what to do: Take $\frac{1}{5}$ of 40, which is 8 caramels. Take $\frac{5}{8}$ of 40, which is 25 butterscotches. The caramels and the butterscotches are 8 + 25 = 33. Subtract that from 40 and you've got the fudge.

7. **A** Plug in. Let $x = 2$. If Dixie spent an average of \$2 a shirt, then she spent a total of \$10 on shirts. Let $y = 4$, and she spent an average of \$4 a hat, for a total of \$12. Our total is 10 + 12 = \$22. Circle that. Now on to the answer choices, and $x = 2$ and $y = 4$. (A) is 5(2) + 3(4) = 22.

HARD

8. **D** First multiply the ratio by something big to get rid of the fraction. Any multiple of 6 and 5 will do. So $30\left(\frac{1}{6}\right) : 30\left(\frac{1}{5}\right) = 5:6$. Now you've got $5:6 = 35:x$. Since 35 is 5×7, x is 6×7, or 42. The new ratio is 35:42, which is the same as 5:6.

9. **B** Write down your ratios and label them neatly. You have

$$\frac{b:y}{3:4} \qquad \frac{r:y}{2:3}$$

If the artist uses equal amounts of blue and red, you have to multiply each ratio so the numbers under b and r are the same:

$$\frac{b:y}{(2)(3:4)} \qquad \frac{r:y}{(2:3)(3)}$$

The result is

$$\frac{b:y}{6:8} \qquad \frac{r:y}{6:9}$$

The yellow is 8 parts + 9 parts = 17 parts, and the total is 6 + 8 + 6 + 9 = 29 parts. On complicated ratio problems, it's important, to organize the information legibly and label everything as you go along, or else you'll find yourself looking at a bunch of meaningless numbers.

10. **C** Plug in the answer choices! Start with (C) If the larger radius is 6, the smaller radius is 2 less than that, or 4. The area of the smaller circle = 16π, and the area of the larger circle is 36π. $16\pi:36\pi$ is a ratio of 4:9. (Just divide the whole ratio by 4) If you picked (E), you must've had a momentary blackout—that answer is way too appealing to be right on a hard question. If you're going to guess, guess something that is not too good to be true.

A shortcut for averages: If the list of numbers is consecutive, consecutive odd, or consecutive even, then the average will be the middle number. (If the list has an even number of elements, you have to average the two middle numbers.) The average will also be the middle number (or average of the two middle numbers) of any list that goes up in consistent increments. For example, the average of 6, 15, 24, 33, and 42 is 24, since the numbers go up in increments of 9.

PROBLEM SET 9: EXPONENTS, ROOTS, AND EQUATIONS

EASY

1. If $t^3 = -8$, then $t^2 =$

   (A) -4
   (B) -2
   (C) 2
   (D) 4
   (E) 8

2. If $60 = (7 + 8)(x - 2)$, then $x =$

   (A) 15
   (B) 10
   (C) 9
   (D) 7
   (E) 6

3. If $4x - 2y = 10$, and $7x + 2y = 23$, what is the value of x ?

   (A) $\dfrac{1}{3}$

   (B) 1

   (C) 3

   (D) 13

   (E) 14

4. For all integers x and y, let

   $\bigstar (x + y) = \dfrac{x^2}{y^2}$. What is the value of

   $\bigstar (2 + y) \times \bigstar (y + 1)$?

   (A) 16
   (B) 9
   (C) 5
   (D) 4
   (E) 3

5. For their science homework, Brenda and Dylan calculated the volume of air that filled a basketball. If the formula for the volume of a sphere is $V = \dfrac{4}{3}\pi r^3$, and the diameter of the basketball was 6, what was the volume of the air inside the basketball?

   (A) 4π
   (B) 14π
   (C) 32π
   (D) 36π
   (E) 72π

6. $\dfrac{\sqrt{a} \cdot \sqrt{b}}{3\sqrt{a} - 2\sqrt{a}} =$

   (A) $\dfrac{\sqrt{b}}{\sqrt{a}}$

   (B) $\sqrt{b}$

   (C) $\dfrac{2\sqrt{a}}{b}$

   (D) $\sqrt{ab}$

   (E) $\sqrt{a^2 b}$

7. On a certain test, Radeesh earned 2 points for every correct answer and lost 1 point for every incorrect answer. If he answered all 30 questions on the test and received a score of 51, how many questions did Radeesh answer *incorrectly*?

(A) 3
(B) 7
(C) 15
(D) 21
(E) 24

HARD

8. If $\frac{1}{2}(z - 4)(z + 4) = m$, then, in term of z, what is the value of $z^2 - 16$?

(A) $\sqrt{m}$

(B) $\frac{m}{2}$

(C) m

(D) $2m$

(E) m^2

9. If $(y + 5)^2 = 49$, then which one of the following could be the value of $(y + 3)^2$?

(A)   1
(B)   49
(C)   64
(D)   81
(E) 225

10. If $a - b = 4$, $b - 6 = c$, $c - 2 = d$, and $a + d = 4$, what is the value of a ?

(A)   4
(B)   8
(C) 12
(D) 16
(E) It cannot be determined from the
     information given.

Answers and Explanations: Problem Set 9

Easy

1. **D** $t = -2$, and $(-2)^2 = 4$.

2. **E** Plug in the answer choices. Try (C) first: $(15)(9 - 2) = (15)(7) = 105$. It should equal 60, so you need a much smaller number. Try (E): $(15)(6 - 2) = (15)(4) = 60$. It works. Or you could solve the equation algebraically:

   $60 = 15(x - 2)$
   $60 = 15x - 30$
   $90 = 15x$
   $6 = x$

3. **C** Stack 'em and add:

   $4x - 2y = 10$

   $7x + 2y = 23$

   $11x = 33$

   $x = 3$

Medium

4. **D** In this function, all you have to do is square the first thing in the parentheses and put it over the square of the second thing in the parentheses. So $(2 + y) = \dfrac{2^2}{y^2}$. And $(y + 1) = \dfrac{y^2}{1}$. Now multiply them. The y^2 cancels, so you get 2^2.

5. **D** Don't worry—you weren't supposed to know this formula. That's why they gave it to you, so don't get freaked out. Just use the information in the question to solve for V. If the diameter of the basketball was 6, the radius was 3:

   $$V = \frac{4}{3}\pi r^3, \text{ so } V = \frac{4}{3}\pi(3^3) = \frac{4}{3}\pi(27) = 36\pi.$$

   You may see some totally unfamiliar formula on the test—physics, for instance—but you don't have to understand the formula or know anything about it. All you have to do is substitute in any value they give you and solve for the variable they ask for.

6. **B** Remember that you can multiply or divide what's under a square root sign and add or subtract when what's under the square root sign is the same. Begin by simplifying the denominator. $\dfrac{\sqrt{a} \bullet \sqrt{b}}{3\sqrt{a} - 2\sqrt{a}} = \dfrac{\sqrt{a} \bullet \sqrt{b}}{\sqrt{a}} = \sqrt{b}$.

7. **A** Plug in the answer choices. If Radeesh got 2 points for every right answer, and the test had 30 questions, the top score was 60. If he got a 51, he did pretty well, so start with (A). (Remember, the answer choices represent the number of questions he answered incorrectly.) If he missed 3, then he got 27 right. $27 \times 2 = 54$. Subtract 3 for 3 wrong answers, and you get 51.

   [Don't worry if you didn't see which answer to start with. If you started with (C), it gave you way too many wrong answers, didn't it? So cross off (C), (D), and (E) and you've only got 2 left to try.]

HARD

8. **D** The easiest way to solve this question is to recognize that $(z - 4)(z + 4) = (z - 16)^2$. This, you can rewrite the initial equation as $\dfrac{1}{2}(z - 16)^2 = m$. Thus, $z - 16^2 = 2m$. Otherwise, plug in. Try $z = 6$, which means $m = 5$. The value of $z^2 - 16$ is 10.

9 **D** You need to do a bit of trial by error here. The easiest value of y is 2. However, 25 is not an answer choice. What other value of y would work? How about -12? That works, and 81 is an answer. If you picked anything else, you made a careless error involving positive and negative signs.

10. **B** Start off by eliminating (E), as that would be too easy for a complicated looking question towards the end. Before you start the lengthy process of substitution, try stack-and-add. You need to bring all of the variables to the left, and all of the numbers to the right, so your stack will look like this:

    $a - b = 4$
    $b - c = 6$
    $c - d = 2$
    $a + d = 4$

    Add everything up. It turns out that b, c, and d disappear, leaving $2a = 16$, or $a = 8$.

PROBLEM SET 10: LINES, ANGLES, AND COORDINATES

EASY

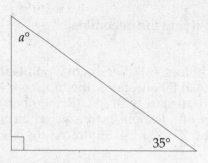

1. In the figure above, $3a - a =$

   (A) 40°
   (B) 55°
   (C) 90°
   (D) 110°
   (E) 165°

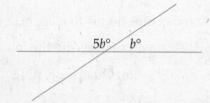

2. In the figure above, $b =$

   (A) 20°
   (B) 30°
   (C) 40°
   (D) 45°
   (E) 180°

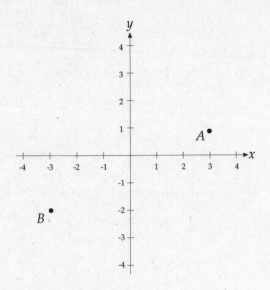

3. The x-coordinate of Point A minus the y-coordinate of Point B equals

(A) −2
(B) −1
(C) 0
(D) 3
(E) 5

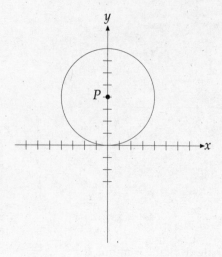

4. Point P is the center of circle Q, which has a

   radius of 4. Which of the following points lies

   on circle Q?

   (A) (4, 0)
   (B) (0, 4)
   (C) (−4, 4)
   (D) (3, 1)
   (E) (4, 3)

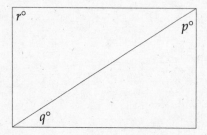

5. In the rectangle above, $p + q - r =$

   (A) 0°
   (B) 15°
   (C) 26°
   (D) 35°
   (E) 50°

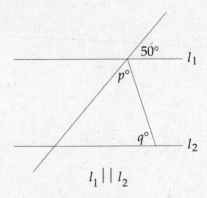

$l_1 \mid\mid l_2$

Note: Figure not drawn to scale.

6. In the figure above, $p + q =$

(A) 180°
(B) 150°
(C) 130°
(D) 90°
(E) 70°

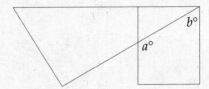

7. The figure above is formed by a triangle overlapping a rectangle. What does $a + b$ equal?

(A) 80°
(B) 90°
(C) 150°
(D) 180°
(E) 270°

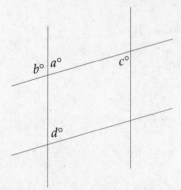

Note: Figure not drawn to scale.

8. Which of the following statements must be true?

   I. $a + b < 180$
   II. $a + d = 180$
   III. $a + d > 180$

   (A) None
   (B) I only
   (C) II only
   (D) I and II only
   (E) II and II only

9. The tick marks on the number line above are equally spaced. If 2 is halfway between b and c, the value of $c - a$ is 10, what is the value of b ?

   (A) − 4
   (B) − 3
   (C) − 2
   (D)   0
   (E)   6

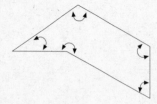

10. What is the total number of degrees of the marked angles?

   (A) 180
   (B) 270
   (C) 360
   (D) 540
   (E) 720

Answers and Explanations: Problem Set 10

Easy

1. **D** A triangle has 180°. So $90 + 35 + a = 180$, and $a = 55$. Plug that into the equation and get $3(55) - 55 = 110$.

2. **B** $5b$ and b lie on a straight line, so $5b + b = 180$ and $b = 30$.

3. **E** The x-coordinate of Point A is 3, and the y-coordinate of Point B is -2. So $3 - (-2) = 5$.

Medium

4. **C** Just plot the points and see which one falls on the circle.

5. **A** As always, mark whatever info you can on your diagram: $r = 90$, and the bottom angle is also 90, because this is a rectangle. $p + q = 90$, because they are the two remaining angles in a right triangle. That means $p + q - r = 0$.

6. **C** Again, mark info on the diagram. The unmarked angle of the triangle is 50° because l_1 and l_2 are parallel, so $50 + p + q = 180$ and $p + q = 130°$. (You can't figure out what p and q are individually, but the question doesn't ask you to.)

7. **D** Estimate first. a is around 130 and b is bigger than 45, so $a + b$ should be a little bigger than 175. Pick (D) and keep cruising. To figure the angles exactly, ignore the triangle and look at the quadrilateral in the bottom half of the rectangle. The angles are $a + b + 90 + 90$. Since a quadrilateral has 360°, $a + b = 180$.

Hard

8. **A** It's important to realize what you *don't* know: Are any of these lines parallel? *You don't know.* So you can't draw any conclusions at all other than the rule that a line contains 180°.

9. **C** The best way to approach this question is to plug in the answers. Suppose b is -2. Because the midpoint between b and c is 2, you can see that each tick mark represents a value of 2 more than the previous tick mark. Thus, a is -4, and c is 6. Now, you have to check this against the remaining information in the question. So $c - a$ must be 10. Is it? Yes, so (C) is our answer!

10. **D** Estimate first and see what you can cross out. Since you have two angles that are bigger than 90 and one angle that's bigger than 180, you should be able at least to cross out (A), (B), and (C). To figure out the exact number of degrees, divide the figure into three triangles:

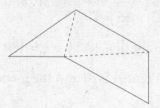

The total degrees will be $180 \times 3 = 540$.

PROBLEM SET 11: TRIANGLES

Easy

1. If the area of the triangle above is 6, what is its perimeter?

   (A) 8
   (B) 11
   (C) 12
   (D) 15
   (E) 16

2. If $x = 3$, what is the area of the triangle above?

   (A) 10
   (B) 12
   (C) 21
   (D) 30
   (E) 45

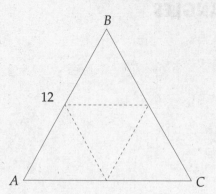

3. If equilateral triangle *ABC* is cut by three lines, as shown, to form four equilateral triangles of equal area, what is the length of a side of 1 of the smaller triangles?

(A) 3
(B) 4
(C) 5
(D) 6
(E) 8

MEDIUM

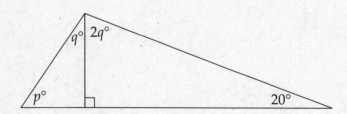

4. What is the value of *p* in the figure above?

(A) 50
(B) 55
(C) 60
(D) 65
(E) 70

5. A movie theater is 3 blocks due north of a supermarket, and a beauty parlor is 4 blocks due east of the movie theater. How many blocks long is the street that runs directly from the supermarket to the beauty parlor?

(A)   2.5
(B)   3
(C)   4
(D)   5
(E)   7

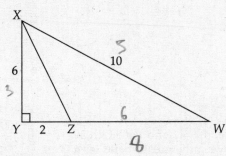

6. What is the area of triangle *WXZ* in the figure above?

(A) 6
(B) 12
(C) 18
(D) 24
(E) 36

HARD

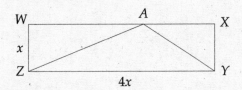

7. In the figure above, what is the area of triangle *YAZ* ?

(A) $3x$
(B) x^2
(C) $5x$
(D) $2x^2$
(E) $4x^2$

8. A square is inscribed in a circle with area 9π. What is the area of the square?

(A) $3\sqrt{2}$

(B) $9\sqrt{2}$

(C) 18

(D) 36

(E) 162

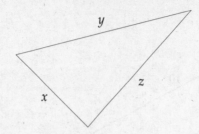

9. In the figure above, if $x = 7$ and $y = 11$, then the difference between the greatest and least possible integer values of z is

(A) 11
(B) 12
(C) 13
(D) 14
(E) 15

10. An equilateral triangle with a perimeter of 12 is inscribed in a circle. What is the area of the circle?

(A) $\sqrt{3}\pi$

(B) $2\sqrt{2}\pi$

(C) $2\sqrt{3}\pi$

(D) 3π

(E) 12π

Answers and Explanations: Problem Set 11

Easy

1. **C** Several ways to get this question: You could recognize that it's a
   Pythagorean triple (3:4:5), which would give you the length of the
   unmarked leg. Or you could set up the following equation:

   $$a = \frac{1}{2}bh$$

   $\frac{1}{2}b(4) = 6$, so $2b = 6$ and $b = 3$. All you did was substitute the height and
   the area, both of which are given in the problem, into the formula for the
   area of a triangle.

2. **E** If $x = 3$, then the base of the triangle is 6 and the height is 15. That
   would mean the area is $\frac{1}{2}(6)(15) = 45$.

3. **D** Each vertex of the small triangles bisects a side of the big triangle, so
   each side is 6. (Don't forget to estimate.)

Medium

4. **B** Start with the triangle to the right of the height line. As the height forms
   an angle of 90 and the given angle is 20, the third angle is 70 (180 − 110).
   Thus, $2q = 70$, and $q = 35$. Now go to the triangle to the left of the height
   line. As the height forms an angle of 90 and q is 35, p is 55.

5. **D** Draw a little map, which should look like this:

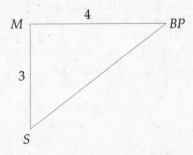

   Now you have a 3:4:5 right triangle, so the street from the supermarket
   to the beauty parlor is 5 blocks long.

6. **C** Use the Pythagorean Theorem to find the base of triangle WYZ: $6^2 + b^2 = 10^2$. The base is 8. (This is the 6-8-10 triple, so you didn't really need to use the Pythagorean Theorem.) As $XY = 2$, the base of triangle WXZ is 6. The height of triangle WXZ is the same as the height of WYZ, also 6. Thus, the area ($\frac{1}{2}bh$) is 18.

HARD

7. **D** Plug in. If $x = 2$, then ZY is 8 and WZ is 2. (Write that on your diagram.) To get the area of YAZ, notice that WZ is the height of the triangle, so $\frac{1}{2}$ (8)(2) = 8. Plug 2 back into the answer choices, and (D) is $2(2^2) = 8$.

8. **C** As there is no diagram, first draw a square in a circle. As the area of the circle is 9π, the radius is 3 as Area $= \pi r^2$. How does this help? Often on the SAT, questions involving squares are really about the diagonal of the square, so draw in the diagonal. The diagonal is the diameter of the circle, so the diagonal is 6. You can use the Pythagorean Theorem or your knowledge of 45-45-90 triangles to figure out the sides. Label the sides of the square x. If you use the Pythagorean Theorem, you will solve $x^2 + x^2 = 6^2$. $x = \sqrt{18}$. If you use the 45-45-90 relationships, you will get $x = \frac{6}{\sqrt{2}}$. Either way, the area of the square is 18.

9. **B** Here's the rule: The sum of any two sides of a triangle must be more than the third side. So if you already have sides of 7 and 11, the longest the third side could be is a little less than 18. Since the third side has to be an integer, the longest it could be is 17. Now for the shortest possible length of the third side: 11 − 7 = 4, so the third side has to be an integer bigger than 4, which is 5. So the difference between the greatest possible and the least possible is 17 − 5 = 12.

10. **A** As there is no diagram, first draw an equilateral triangle in a circle. As the perimeter of the triangle is 12, each side is 4. However, you need the radius of the circle. Draw in the height of the triangle. This is the diameter of the circle. The height cuts the bottom side in half, so you can solve for the height using the Pythagorean Theorem or your knowledge of 30-60-90 triangles. (Often on the SAT, questions about equilateral triangles are really about 30-60-90 triangles.) If you use the Pythagorean Theorem, you will solve $2^2 + h^2 = 4^2$. $x = 2\sqrt{3}$. If you use the 30-60-90 relationships, you will get the same result. Thus the radius of the circle (half the diameter) is $\sqrt{3}$. Using the formula for area of a circle Area = πr^2, you get 3π.

PROBLEM SET 12: CIRCLES, QUADRILATERALS, BOXES, AND CANS

EASY

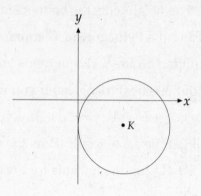

1. Point *K* is the center of the circle above, and the coordinates of Point *K* are (2, –1). What is the area of the circle?

   (A) π
   (B) 2π
   (C) 4π
   (D) 6π
   (E) 8π

2. Circle *P* has a radius of 7, and Circle *R* has a diameter of 8. The circumference of Circle *P* is how much greater than the circumference of Circle *R* ?

   (A) π
   (B) 6π
   (C) 8π
   (D) 16π
   (E) 33π

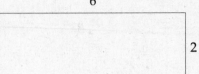

6

2

3. How many squares with sides of 1 could fit into the rectangle above?

   (A) 3
   (B) 4
   (C) 6
   (D) 9
   (E) 12

MEDIUM

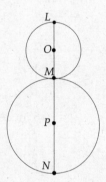

4. In the figure above, LM is $\frac{1}{3}$ of LN. If the radius of the circle with center P is 6, what is the area of the circle with center O ?

   (A) 4π
   (B) 9π
   (C) 12π
   (D) 18π
   (E) 36π

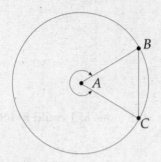

5. In the figure above, the circle has center A, and $BC = AB$. What is the degree measure of the marked angle?

(A) 60°
(B) 180°
(C) 270°
(D) 300°
(E) 340°

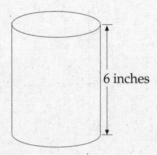

6 inches

6. In the figure above, the radius of the base of the cylinder is half its height. What is the volume of the cylinder in cubic inches?

(A) 9π
(B) 15π
(C) 18π
(D) 36π
(E) 54π

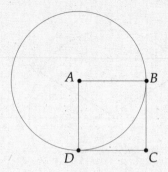

7. Points *D* and *B* lie on the circle above with center *A*. If square *ABCD* has an area of 16, what is the length of arc *BD* ?

   (A) 2π
   (B) 4
   (C) 8
   (D) 4π
   (E) 8π

HARD

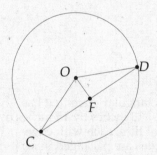

8. In the figure above, what is the circumference of the circle with center *O*, if *COD* is 120° and *OF* bisects *CD* and has a length of 1.5 ?

   (A) $\dfrac{2\pi}{3}$

   (B) $\dfrac{3\pi}{2}$

   (C) 3π

   (D) 6π

   (E) 9π

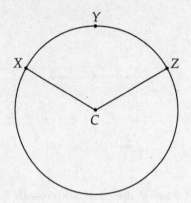

9. In the figure above, C is the center of a circle. If the length of the arc XYZ is 4π, what is the radius of the circle?

(A) 4

(B) $2\sqrt{3}$

(C) 6

(D) $2\sqrt{4}$

(E) 12

10. Jeremy will fill a rectangular crate that has inside dimensions of 18 inches by 15 inches by 9 inches with cubical tiles, each with edge lengths of 3. If the tiles are packaged in sets of 8, how many packages will Jeremy need to completely fill the crate?

(A) 11
(B) 12
(C) 90
(D) 101
(E) 102

Answers and Explanations: Problem Set 12

Easy

1. **C** Count up the units of the radius—it's 2. Then use the formula for area of a circle: $\pi r^2 = \pi(2^2) = 4\pi$.

2. **B** The circumference of Circle P is $2\pi r = 2\pi(7) = 14$. The circumference of Circle R is $2\pi r = 2\pi(4) = 8\pi$. Now just subtract. If you picked (E), you calculated area instead of circumference.

3. **E** Drawing on the diagram could help. How many sides of 1 can fit along the long edge of the rectangle? 6. And how many rows will fit along the short edge? 2. Now just multiply $6 \times 2 = 12$. Or draw them in and count them up.

Medium

4. **B** Write in 6 by the radius of the bigger circle. That makes the diameter of the bigger circle 12. If LM (the diameter of the smaller circle) is $\frac{1}{3}$ the length of LN, the equation is $\left(\frac{1}{3}\right)(12 + x) = x$. $4 = x - \frac{x}{3}$, and $x = 6$. (You don't have to write an equation. You could estimate and try some numbers. Doesn't LM look like it's about half of MN? It is.) If the diameter of the smaller circle is 6, then its radius is 3 and its area is 9.

5. **D** Estimate first. The marked angle is way more than 180—in fact, it's not that far from 360. Cross out (A) and (B). You know $AC = AB$ because they're both radii. That means $BC = AB = AC$, and that triangle is equilateral. So angle BAC is 60°. Subtract that from 360 and you're in business. (Even if all you could do was estimate, go ahead and take a guess.)

6. **E** If the radius is half the height, then the radius is 3. To get the volume of a cylinder, multiply the area of the base times the height—in this case, $\pi(3^2) \times 6 = 54\pi$.

7. **A** If the square has an area of 16, then the side of the square is 4. Write that on your diagram. Now you know the radius of the circle is also 4, so the circumference is 8π. Angle *BAD* has 90°, since it's a corner of the square. And since 90 is $\frac{1}{4}$ of 360, arc *BD* is $\frac{1}{4}$ of the circumference. So arc *BD* is $\left(\frac{1}{4}\right)(8\pi)$, or 2π. If you estimated first, as we hope you did, you could have crossed out (D) and (E), and maybe even (C).

HARD

8. **D** Write the info on your diagram. If *OF* bisects *CD*, it also bisects angle *COD*, making two 60° angles. Now there are two 30:60:90 triangles. If the shortest leg of one of those triangles is 1.5, then the hypotenuse is 2 × 1.5, or 3. Aha! That distance is also the radius of the circle, so the circumference is 6π.

9. **C** The ratio of the length of an arc to the circumference of the circle is the same as the ratio of the degree measure of the arc to the 360 degrees of the circle. As 120 degrees is one-third of the circle, the length of the arc is one-third of the circumference. Thus, the circumference of the circle is 12π. As Circumference = $2\pi r$, the radius is 6.

10. **B** To find the number of tiles that will fit in the crate, you must divide the dimensions of the crate by all three dimensions of the tiles:

$$\frac{18 \times 15 \times 9}{3 \times 3 \times 3} = 90$$

But don't select 90 as your answer! The question asks how many packages of 8 tiles are needed. So, divide 90 by 8, which equals 11 plus a remainder. As 11 packages will contain only 88 of the 90 tiles needed, Jeremy must buy a 12th package.

> One more thing: Circle questions tend to appear most often in the late-medium and hard questions.

PROBLEM SET 13: FUNCTIONS, CHARTS, AND GRAPHS

EASY

	Original Price	Sale Price
Store *A*	$25	$20
Store *B*	$20	$15
Store *C*	$30	$25
Store *D*	$35	$30

1. The chart above shows the original and sale prices of a certain item at each of four different stores. Which of the following stores provides a discount of 20% or more on this item?

    I.   Store *A*
   II.   Store *B*
  III.   Store C

(A) I only
(B) II only
(C) III only
(D) I and II only
(E) I and III only

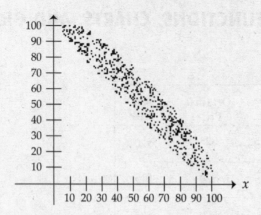

2. Which of the following is mostly likely the slope of the line of best fit for the scatterplot above?

    (A) −10
    (B) −1
    (C)   0
    (D)   1
    (E) 10

3. If $f(x) = 2x + 1$ and $f(a) = 2$, what is the value of a ?

    (A) −2

    (B) $-\dfrac{1}{2}$

    (C) $\dfrac{1}{2}$

    (D) 2

    (E) 5

4. If $f(x) = 4x + 2$, which of the following is the graph of $f(x)$?

(A)
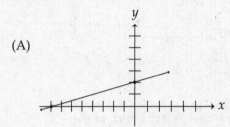

(B)
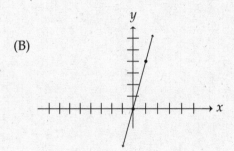

(C)
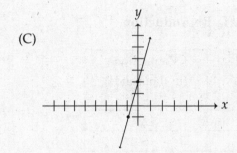

(D)
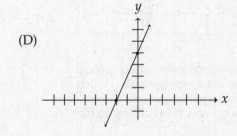

(E)
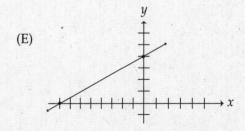

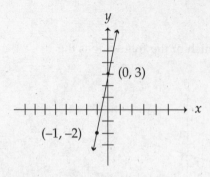

5. If the graph above is that of $f(x)$, which of the following could be $f(x)$?

(A) $f(x) = \dfrac{1}{5}x + \dfrac{1}{3}$

(B) $f(x) = \dfrac{1}{5}x + 3$

(C) $f(x) = \dfrac{1}{3}x + 5$

(D) $f(x) = 3x + 5$

(E) $f(x) = 5x + 3$

Bacteria Reproduction

Time (in seconds) t	Population (in thousands) p
1	2
2	6
3	18
4	54

6. The table above shows the population growth of a certain bacteria over four seconds. Which one of the following equations shows the relationship between t and p, according to the table?

(A) $p = 3t$
(B) $p = 2t^2$
(C) $p = 9(t + 2)$
(D) $p = 2 \times 3^t$
(E) $p = 2 \times 3^{(t-1)}$

Elevator Usage

Date	Number of uses
March 31	837
April 30	1,347
May 31	2,142
June 30	2,799
July 31	2,824
August 31	3,002

7. The table above shows the total number of times a certain elevator has been used by the end of the last day of each of six consecutive months. Local regulations require that the elevator undergo an inspection every 2,000 uses or every 4 calendar months, whichever occurs first. If an inspection took place on January 31, when was the next inspection required?

(A) April 30
(B) May 31
(C) June 30
(D) July 31
(E) August 31

HARD

$$y = f(x)$$

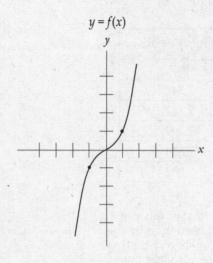

8. If the graph above shows the function $f(x) = x^3$, which one of the following graphs shows $f(x) = (x + 2)^3 - 3$?

(A)

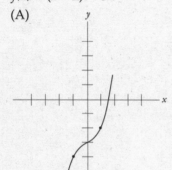

(B)

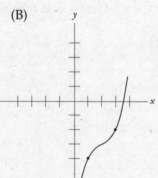

(C)

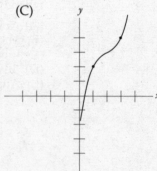

(D)

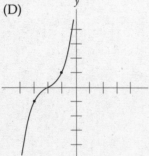

(E)

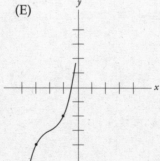

9. The function g is defined as $g(x) = \dfrac{x^2}{3 - |x - 4|}$.
For which values of x is $g(x)$ NOT defined?

(A) $x = 1$ and $x = 3$
(B) $x = 4$ and $x = 7$
(C) $x = 3$ and $x = 4$
(D) $x = 3$ and $x = 7$
(E) $x = 1$ and $x = 7$

10. For all positive integers a and b, let $a \leftrightarrow b$ be defined by $a \leftrightarrow b = a^2 - b^a$. What is the value of $(2 \leftrightarrow 3) - (1 \leftrightarrow 2)$?

(A) -6
(B) -4
(C) 0
(D) 4
(E) 6

ANSWERS AND EXPLANATIONS: PROBLEM SET 13

EASY

1. **D** Remember that the formula for percent change is $\dfrac{difference}{original} \times 100$. The discount at Store A is $\dfrac{5}{25} \times 100 = 20\%$, and the discount at Store B is $\dfrac{5}{20} \times 100 = 25\%$. On the other hand, the discounts at Stores C and D, respectively, are $\dfrac{5}{30} \times 100 = 16.67\%$ and $\dfrac{5}{35} \times 100 = 14.29\%$. Thus, only Stores A and B have discounts of 20% or greater.

2. **B** Draw a line that connects most of the points. It is a straight line that goes down from right to left, which means it has a negative slope. Only (A) and (B) are negative slopes. Eyeball the line to see that it is not very steep. So, the slope is closer to 1 than 10. Alternatively, you could find points and ballpark the slope. The line roughly includes (50, 50), so the rise and run are the same. Therefore, the slope is –1.

3. **C** If $f(a) = 2a + 1$, and $f(a) = 2$, that means $2 = 2a + 1$. Subtract 1 from both sides to get $1 = 2a$. Divide both sides by 2 to find $a = \dfrac{1}{2}$.

MEDIUM

4. **C** Don't do a lot of formula work. Think about how graphs work. In the equation, 2 represents the y-intercept, so eliminate any graphs that do not cross the y-axis at 2. You are down to (A) and (C). A slope of greater than 1 is relatively steep as compared to a 45-degree angle, while a fractional slope is relatively shallow. The slope here is 4, so you need a steep graph. Eliminate (A), and the answer is (C).

5. **E** Don't do a lot of formula work. Think about how graphs work. The y-intercept on the graph is 3, so you need a formula that ends in + 3. Eliminate (A), (C), and (D). A slope of greater than 1 is relatively steep as compared to a 45-degree angle, while a fractional slope is relatively shallow. The slope of the lines on the graph is relatively steep, so eliminate (B), and the answer is (E).

6. **E** Don't try to figure this one out by deriving an equation. Plug in by testing the numbers in the table against the functions in the answer choices. Only (E) is satisfied by all the data in the table.

7. **D** This question is a bit complicated to read, but once you understand what it is asking, the process is not difficult. To find out whether 2,000 uses or 4 months occurred first, check July (4 months after the previous inspection) first. If there have not yet been 2,000 uses, then that is your answer. If there have been more than 2,000 uses, you need to check June (and possibly earlier) to find out when 2,000 uses first occurred. As of July 31, there were 2,824 total uses. On March 31, there were 837 uses. The difference (1,987) is less than 2,000, so the 4-month period occurred first. If you picked (C), you didn't understand the table: the numbers are total uses, not the number of uses in that month.

HARD

8. **E** The easiest way to handle this is to understand how functions move. The – 3 outside the parentheses shifts the original graph down by 3 units. Eliminate (C) and (D) because they are not shifted down. The + 2 inside the parentheses shifts the original graph to the left by 2 units. Eliminate (A) and (B) because they are not shifted to the left. You can also plug in, testing one of the points indicated by a dot against the function you are looking for.

9. **E** The function will not be defined when the denominator is equal to 0. If you don't want to analyze the denominator to determine when it would equal 0, you can plug in the answers. Even though the answers are not in ascending or descending order, you can still start with (C). If you plug 3 into the denominator, you do not get zero, so eliminate (C) and anything else with 3: (A) and (D). Notice that both of the remaining answers have 7, so there's no need to test it. Try 1 in (E). You get 0, so that's your answer.

10. **B** When you see a weird symbol, it's really just a function question, so just follow the instructions. In this case, you are told that when you see numbers on either side of the arrow symbol, you square the first number and subtract from the value obtained when you raise the second number to the power of the first number. The tricky part here is making sure you follow PEMDAS and distribute your negative signs properly. Your work should look like this:

$$(2 \leftrightarrow 3) - (1 \leftrightarrow 2) = (2^2 - 3^2) - (1^2 - 2^1)$$
$$(4 - 9) - (1 - 2)$$
$$-5 - (-1) = -4$$

PROBLEM SET 14: MIXED BAG

EASY

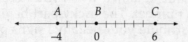

1. On the number line above, what is
   $BC - AB$?

   (A) 0
   (B) 2
   (C) 4
   (D) 6
   (E) 10

2. If n and s are integers, and $n + 5 < 7$, and
   $s - 6 < -4$, which of the following could be a
   value of $n + s$?

   (A) 2
   (B) 3
   (C) 4
   (D) 6
   (E) 9

3. A, B, C, and D lie on a line. The distance
   between A and B is 12. Point B is the midpoint
   of AD, and point C is the midpoint of AB. What
   is the distance between C and D ?

   (A) 6
   (B) 12
   (C) 18
   (D) 24
   (E) 36

MEDIUM

4. Which of the following lines is perpendicular to
   $y = 2x + 7$?

   (A) $y = 3x + \dfrac{1}{7}$

   (B) $y = 3x - \dfrac{1}{7}$

   (C) $y = -\dfrac{1}{2}x + 3$

   (D) $y = \dfrac{1}{2}x + 3$

   (E) $y = \dfrac{1}{2}x + 7$

5. If S is the set of the prime factors of n, and R is the set of the prime factors of $2n$, how many more numbers does set R contain than set S ?

(A) $2n$
(B) n
(C) 2
(D) 1
(E) 0

6. In a recent marathon, 70 percent of those who entered the race reached the finish line. If 7,200 did not reach the finish line, how many people entered the race?

(A)   9,360
(B) 12,240
(C) 16,800
(D) 21,000
(E) 24,000

HARD

7. What is the area of an equilateral triangle with a side length of 10 ?

(A) 25
(B) $25\sqrt{2}$
(C) $25\sqrt{3}$
(D) 50
(E) $50\sqrt{3}$

8. Point A (x, y), where x and y are negative numbers, is reflected about the x-axis to Point B, and Point B is then reflected about the x-axis to Point C. In terms of x and y, what is the sum of the coordinates about the y-axis to Point C ?

(A) $x + y$
(B) $x - y$
(C) $-x + y$
(D) $-x - y$
(E) $2x + 2y$

9. When positive integer a is divided by 5, the remainder is 3. When positive integer b is divided by 5, the remainder is 4. What is the remainder when the product ab is divided by 5 ?

(A) 0
(B) 1
(C) 2
(D) 3
(E) 4

10. A four-digit number is formed such that the units digit is 3, the thousands digit is 5, and the tens and hundreds digits are different from each (but may be the same as either the units or thousands digit). How many different numbers can be created?

(A)   56
(B)   90
(C)   100
(D) 1,350
(E) 9,000

Answers and Explanations: Problem Set 14

Easy

1. **B** BC has a length of 6. AB has a length of 4. So $BC - AB = 2$.

> On number line problems, sometimes you want the distance between 2 points, as in the problem above. And sometimes you want the number of a point on the line—for instance, using this number line, $A + B = -4$, because $A = -4$ and $B = 0$. You can have a negative value for a point on the line, but not a negative distance. Read the problem carefully and mark up your diagram so you don't confuse the two.

2. **A** First fix the ranges. You can see $n < 2$ and $s < 2$. Since they both must be integers, the greatest either n or s could be is 1. $1 + 1$ is 2, so that is the only answer that works.

3. **C** The easiest way to solve this problem is to draw a number line. Say that point A is at 0 on the number line and that B is at 12. Since 6 is the midpoint of AB, this puts C at 6. Therefore, the distance between C and D is 24 − 6, or 18.

MEDIUM

4. **C** In the form $y = mx + b$, m is the slope, which means that the line given by the equation $y = 2x + 7$ has a slope of 2. A line perpendicular to $y = 2x + 7$ will have a slope that is the negative reciprocal to 2. (C) has a slope of $-\frac{1}{2}$.

5. **D** Plug in. Try $n = 10$. The prime factors of 10 are 2 and 5. It has 2 prime factors. $2n = 20$. The prime factors of 20 are 2, 2, and 5. It has 3 prime factors. 20 has 1 more prime factor than 10. Plug $n = 10$ into the answers to find 1. Only (D) works.

> These questions are a bummer because sometimes it's hard to know where to begin. If you don't see any starting point, just try some numbers and see what happens. If you try a couple of different things and nothing seems to work, skip the question and come back to it later. These questions appear most often in the easy and medium sections. Depending on how the question is asked, you may be able to plug in.

6. **E** You can plug in the answers, starting with (C). If 16,800 entered the race and 70% crossed the finish line, then 11,760 would have crossed the finish line. This leaves 5,040 who did not cross the finish line, which is too low. (E) works.

HARD

7. **C** In order to find the area, you need to find the height first. It's important to draw a picture. When you draw in the height, notice that it makes a 30-60-90 triangle, with the hypotenuse as 10, and the short side as 5. This must mean that the other side (the height) is $5\sqrt{3}$. Just remember that the area formula is: $\frac{1}{2} b \times h$, so it is $\frac{1}{2} \times 10 \times 5\sqrt{3} = 25\sqrt{3}$.

8. **D** Draw the graph and plug in. You know that x and y must both be negative, so make $x = -2$ and $y = -3$. Draw point A at $(-2, -3)$. A reflection creates a mirror image across the axis. So, when Point A reflects across the x axis to Point B in the second quadrant, the coordinates will be $(-2, 3)$. Next, we reflect that point across the y axis to Point C. Here, the mirror image will be $(2, 3)$. The question asks for the sum of these points, so our target answer is 5. Be very careful with your negative signs as you test the answers. (A) = –5. (B) = 1. (C) = –1. (D) = 5. (E) = –10. Thus, (D) is your answer.

9. **C** You can plug in. Pick a number that, when divided by 5, gives a remainder of 3. The first (and easiest) such number is 8. Now pick a number that, when divided by 5, gives a remainder of 4. How about 9? Now find the product, which is 72. When 72 is divided by 5, the remainder is 2.

10. **B** In an arrangements question, first create placeholders. As there are four digits, create four placeholders:

   __ __ __ __

Consider the thousands digit. Because the number for that digit is given, we have only 1 possible choice for that digit. So, put a 1 in the placeholder, and do the same for the units digit, which is also restricted to one choice:

   <u>1</u> __ __ <u>1</u>

It is important not to put the actual numbers—just the quantity of available choices—in the slots, as we will multiply soon. Now, let's take one of the other digits; it doesn't matter which one, so let's use the tens. As the tens digit may repeat numbers already used in the ones and thousands digit, we have 10 options (0, 1, 2, 3, 4, 5, 6, 7, 8, and 9) to choose from. So, put 10 in the placeholder.

   <u>1</u> __ <u>10</u> <u>1</u>

For the hundreds digit, we are told that it may repeat numbers from the ones and thousands digits but not from the tens digit, so we have only 9 numbers to choose from. So, our complete placeholder row looks like this:

   <u>1</u> <u>9</u> <u>10</u> <u>1</u>

Last step: multiply. That's it!

PROBLEM SET 15: GRID-INS

EASY

1. If $x - y = -6$, then y is how much greater than x?

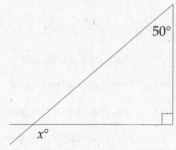

2. In the figure above, what is the value of x?

3. A certain solution requires $3\frac{1}{2}$ grams of additive for each 7 liters of water. At this rate, how many grams of additive should be used with 11 liters of water?

MEDIUM

4. On a number line, the number q is the midpoint between 4 and 7. What is the value of $|2 - q|$?

5. If $\left(\dfrac{x+2}{y+2}\right) = \dfrac{3}{4}$, then what is the value of

$\left(\dfrac{2+y}{2+x}\right)^2$?

6. The speed, in miles per hour, of a particular experimental spacecraft t minutes after it is launched is modeled by the function M, which is defined as $M(t) = 200(3)^{\frac{t}{3}}$. According to this model, what is the speed, in miles per hour, 9 minutes after the spacecraft is launched?

HARD

CLIMATE PREFERENCES

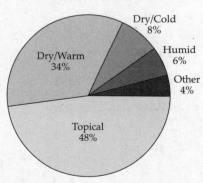

7. The graph above shows the results of a survey in which adults were asked to name their first preference among various types of climates. Of the adults surveyed, a total of 280 answered "Humid" or "Other." How many answered "Other" in the survey?

$-4, 0, 2, 3$

8. A sequence of numbers is formed by repeating the set of numbers until 80 numbers have been listed. What is the sum of the first 31 terms of the sequence?

9. In the figure below, rectangle *LMNO* has dimensions of 18 by 8. Segments *PQ* and *RS* are diagonals of the squares shown. What is the area of the shaded region?

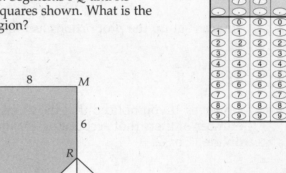

```
L        8        M
6                 6
    P        R
        Q    S
6                 6
O        8        N
```

10. The integer *a* is the product of three consecutive positive integers less than 12. The integer *b* is the product of three consecutive positive integers less than 8. What is the greatest possible value of $\dfrac{b}{a}$?

Answers and Explanations: Problem Set 15

Easy

1. **6**

   Set the equation equal to y, since that's what the question asks for. You get $-y = -6 - x$. Multiply through by -1 and you get $y = 6 + x$, so the answer is 6. For an easier solution, you could also plug in here: Say $x = 2$ and $y = 8$, which satisfies the equation. Then y is equal to x plus 6.

2. **140**

   The unmarked angle in the triangle is 40°, since triangles have 180° and the other angles are 50° and 90°. The 40° angle and x lie on a straight line, so $40 + x = 180$, and $x = 140$.

3. **5.5**

   You can set up the proportions as follows and cross-multiply:

   $$\frac{3.5g}{7l} = \frac{x}{11l}$$

   However, if you noticed that the number of grams is one-half the number of liters (not accounting for units), then all you need to do is divide 11 by 2.

Medium

4. **3.5**

   Draw the number line and identify that midpoint is 5.5. You can also find the midpoint by calculating the average of 4 and 7. The absolute value of $2 - 5.5$ is 3.5.

5. $\dfrac{16}{9}$

   This is a good example of plugging in on a grid-in question. If you make $x = 1$ and $y = 2$, the equation will work:

   $$\left(\frac{1+2}{2+2}\right) = \frac{3}{4}$$

   Now it is easy to solve the problem. By the way, if you noticed that $\left(\dfrac{2+y}{2+x}\right)$ is the reciprocal of $\left(\dfrac{x+2}{y+2}\right)$, you didn't need to plug in. Just square $\dfrac{4}{3}$!

6. **1800**

   This question asks you to plug $t = 9$ into the given formula:

   $$M(t) = 200(3)^{\frac{9}{3}} = 200(3)^3 = 200(9) = 1800.$$

HARD

7. **112**

   Make sure you understand the information you are given and the information you need to find before trying to answer the question. There are 280 people who answered "Humid" or "Other," not 280 total people, so don't take 10 percent of 280. Also, there is no need to calculate the total number of people surveyed. Of the people who answered "Humid" and "Other," 4 out of 10 answered "Other." Thus, the number of people who answer "Other" is $\frac{4}{10}$ of 280, or 112.

8. **5**

   If you are stumped here, you can always type the pattern into your calculator and find the answer. However, on pattern questions, once you understand how the pattern operates, you can arrive at the answer faster. Here, add up the first four numbers of the repeating sequence. They add up to 1. Thus, every time you add another set of the sequence, the total sum will increase by 1. Because you are interested in the first 31 terms of the sequence, there will be 7 complete sets (the first 28 terms) added together and then part of a set (the remaining 3 terms). Those 7 complete sets will add up to 7. So now add in $- 4$, 0, and 2.

9. **126**

Without answer choices, it's tough to ballpark, so you need to slog through! The area of the entire rectangle is 144 (18 × 8). Now you need to find the area of the triangles inside of the rectangle. You can see that the measurements on either side of the squares are all 6 and the entire length of the rectangle is 18, so the portion of the rectangle inside each square is also 6. When a square is cut in half along its diagonal, two 45-45-90 triangles are created. If you don't know how 45-45-90 triangles work, you can look up the ratio in the formula box at the beginning of the section. If each side of the triangle (here the sides of the square) is x, the hypotenuse (here, the diagonal) is $x\sqrt{2}$. Thus, here $6 = x\sqrt{2}$, so $x = \dfrac{6}{\sqrt{2}}$. Now that you have the sides of the squares, you can find the areas of the squares: $\dfrac{6}{\sqrt{2}} \times \dfrac{6}{\sqrt{2}} = \dfrac{36}{2} = 18$. Because the two triangles inside the rectangle add up to one square, you can subtract 18 from 144 to find the area of the shaded region.

10. **35**

Before you engage in a lot of trial by error, think about what will make $\dfrac{b}{a}$ as large as possible. If you have the largest possible b and the smallest possible a, you will have the largest possible $\dfrac{b}{a}$. As b is the product of three consecutive positive integers less than 8, calculate b as 5 × 6 × 7. As a is the product of three consecutive positive integers less than 12, calculate a as 1 × 2 × 3 = 6. Thus, $\dfrac{b}{a} = \dfrac{5 \times 6 \times 7}{6} = 35$.

PROBLEM SET 16: MORE GRID-INS

Easy

1. If $2x - 3y = 7$ and $y = 3$, then what is the value of x?

2. In the figure above, if $a = 170$, what is the value of b?

3. At a certain beach, the cost of renting a beach umbrella is $4.25 per day or $28.00 per week. If Kelly and Brandon rent a beach umbrella for 2 weeks instead of renting one each day for 14 days, how much money, in dollars, will they save? (Leave off the dollar sign when gridding in your answer.)

MEDIUM

4. The average (arithmetic mean) of 8 numbers is 65. If one of the numbers, 65, is removed, what is the average of the remaining 7 numbers?

5. The face of a wall measures 30 yards by 24 yards. If the wall is to be completely covered with square bricks measuring 3 yards on each side, how many bricks will be needed to cover the wall?

All even integers that are not multiples of 4 must be multiples of 6.

6. What is one possible number between 24 and 42 that proves that the statement above is FALSE?

HARD

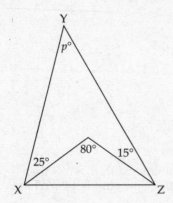

Note: Figure not drawn to scale.

7. In Triangle XYZ above, what is the value of p ?

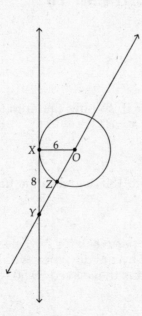

8. In the figure above, O is the center of the circle, the length of segment XY is 8, and the line passing through points X and Y is tangent to the circle at point X. What is the length of segment ZY ?

9. Let the function g be defined as $g(x) = -3x + 6$. If $g(6) = r$, what is the value of $g(r)$?

10. When a number is subtracted from 8 less than three times the number, the result is 142. What is the number?

ANSWERS AND EXPLANATIONS: PROBLEM SET 16

EASY

1. **8**

   The problem tells you that $y = 3$, so plug that into the equation and you get $2x - 9 = 7$. So $2x = 16$ and $x = 8$.

2. **10**

   Write $170°$ next to a. There are 180 degrees in a line, so $b = 10$.

3. **3.50**

   Kelly and Brandon spent $28 per week for 2 weeks for a total of $56. If they had rented the umbrella by the day, they would've spent $14 \times \$4.25$ for a total of $59.50. That means they saved $59.50 - 56 = 3.50$.

MEDIUM

4. **65**

   You can use the average pie. 8 (the number of items) times 65 (the average) gives you a sum of 520. If you subtract 65, the new sum is 455. Divide 455 by 7 (the new number of items) to get the new average: 65. You can also think about this logically: if all 8 numbers were 65, and we removed one of the numbers, the remaining 7 numbers would still average 65.

5. **80**

To find out how many bricks will fit on the wall, you need to divide the dimensions of the wall by the dimensions of the bricks:

$$\frac{30 \times 24}{3 \times 3}$$

6. **26, 34, or 38**

Make sure you understand exactly what the question is asking. First, you need to find a number in the range that is *not* a multiple of 4. Thus, to prove that the statement is false, you need to make sure that the number is also not a multiple of 6. It may be useful to list out all of the numbers—just the even ones, as that is part of the statement, and not 24 or 32, as the question did not say "inclusive":

26, 28, 30, 32, 34, 36, 38, 40

Now, eliminate all those that are multiples of 4:

26, ~~28~~, 30, ~~32~~, 34, ~~36~~, 38, ~~40~~

Next, you need to eliminate any remaining numbers that are divisible by 6:

26, ~~30~~, 34, 38

Any of the three numbers that remain prove the statement false and will be an acceptable answer.

HARD

7. **40**

This figure is not drawn to scale, so be careful as you fill in the information you need. In order to find the value of p, you need to find the sum of angles YXZ and YZX. You are given some information about those angles: the measurements 25 and 15 above the smaller triangle. However, because the figure is not drawn to scale, there is no way to determine the missing measurements—but that does not matter. We don't care what angles YXZ and YZX actually are. We just care about their sum. So, let's look at the smaller triangle. The top vertex is 80, which means that the sum of the bottom vertices is 100. So, plug in, such as 50 and 50. Now we have measures for YXZ and YZX: 75 and 65, for a sum of 140. Subtract that from 180 to find angle p.

8. **4**

To get this question right, you need to know that a line tangent to a circle forms a right angle with the radius at the point of tangency. Thus, triangle *XOY* is a right triangle. You can use the Pythagorean Theorem or recognize the 6-8-10 triangle to find that the hypotenuse is 10. You're not done yet, though. To find *YZ*, you need to subtract the length of *OZ* from 10. *OZ* is a radius, just as is *OX*. As *OX* is 6, so is *OZ*, leaving 4 for *YZ*.

9. **42**

When you are given a function, always take the number inside the parentheses and plug it into the function. Here, you must plug 6 into the function:

$$g(6) = -3(6) + 6 = -18 + 16 = -12$$

Thus $r = -12$. Are you worried that there is no way to grid in a negative number? Actually, you are not done. The question asks for $g(r)$, not $g(6)$. Now that we know $r = -12$, you can plug that number into the function:

$$g(-12) = -3(-12) + 6 = 36 + 6 = 42$$

10. **125**

You need to translate English into Math. Let's call "a number" *x*. You need to subtract *x* from 8 less than 3 times *x*. Three times *x* is $3x$. To find the number 8 less than $3x$, you need to subtract 8. Thus, putting it all together, you get:

$$(3x - 8) - x$$

You are told that the result of this operation is 142, so:

$$(3x - 8) - x = 142$$

Now, you can solve for *x*:

$$2x - 8 = 142$$
$$2x = 150$$
$$x = 125$$

PROBLEM SET 17: MORE MIXED BAG

EASY

1. If $x = 14 - y$, what is 3x when $y = 11$?

    (A) − 9
    (B) − 3
    (C)   3
    (D)   6
    (E)   9

2. At Rose's Flower Shop, the cost of purchasing
    a bundle of 8 ferns is $57. The cost of each
    fern, when purchased separately, is $9. How
    much money would be saved by purchasing a
    bundle of 8 ferns, rather than purchasing 8 ferns
    separately?

    (A) 12
    (B) 13
    (C) 14
    (D) 15
    (E) 16

3. In isosceles triangle ABC, one angle measures
    55 degrees and another angle measures 70
    degrees? Which one of the following is the
    measure of the third angle?

    (A) 40
    (B) 55
    (C) 65
    (D) 70
    (E) It cannot be determined from the information given.

MEDIUM

4. If $24b^2 - 4x = 32$, what is the value of $6b^2 - x$?

    (A)   4
    (B)   6
    (C)   8
    (D) 12
    (E) 16

5. Sasha has a collection of 60 vinyl records, some of which are classic jazz and the rest of which are hip hop. If Sasha has $\frac{1}{4}$ as many classic jazz records as she has hip hop records, how many classic jazz records does she have?

    (A) 12
    (B) 15
    (C) 30
    (D) 45
    (E) 48

6. If p is an integer such that $-5 < p < 5$ and $q = 3p - p^3$, what is the least possible value of q ?

    (A) −76
    (B) −52
    (C) −28
    (D) −4
    (E) 0

HARD

7. In terms of x, what is the difference between $6x + 9$ and $2x - 4$, if $x > 2$?

    (A) $3x + 5$
    (B) $4x - 5$
    (C) $4x + 5$
    (D) $4x + 13$
    (E) $5x - 13$

8. In triangle ABC, the measures of angles a, b, and c, respectively, are in the ratio 2:3:4. What is the value of angle b ?

    (A) 20
    (B) 40
    (C) 60
    (D) 80
    (E) 100

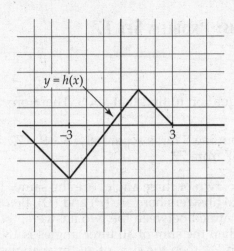

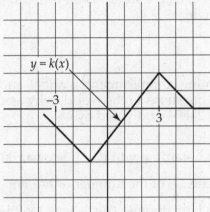

9. The graphs above show the complete functions
   h and k. Which one of the following expresses
   $k(x)$ in terms of $h(x)$?

   (A) $k(x) = h(x) + 2$
   (B) $k(x) = h(x) - 2$
   (C) $k(x) = h(x + 2)$
   (D) $k(x) = h(x - 2)$
   (E) $k(x) = 2h(x)$

10. If $h^{\frac{2}{3}} = k^2$, then in terms of k, what is the value of
    h^2 ?

    (A) $k^{\frac{2}{3}}$

    (B) $k^{\frac{4}{9}}$

    (C) k^3

    (D) k^4

    (E) k^6

ANSWERS AND EXPLANATIONS: PROBLEM SET 17

EASY

1. **E** Plug $y = 11$ into the equation to find that $x = 3$. Therefore, $3x = 9$.

2. **D** Calculate the cost of buying 8 ferns separately: $8 \times 9 = 72$. Now, subtract the package price of 57 from 72.

3. **B** In an isosceles triangle, two of three angles are the same. Thus, the only two possible numerical answers here are (B) and (D). Before you decide that it cannot be determined between the two answers, try them out. If the third angle is 55, then the sum of all three angles is 180. That works. But if the third angle is 70, then the sum of all three angles is 195, which is not possible in a triangle.

MEDIUM

4. **D** Before you start performing complex manipulations and calculations, ask yourself "Of all the questions in the world, why ask for $6b^2 - x$?" The answer is: $6b^2 - x$ is just $24b^2 - 4x$ divided by 4!

5. **A** Plug in the answers here, starting with (C). If she has 30 classic jazz albums and this represents $\frac{1}{4}$ of the number of hip hop albums she has, she would have 120 hip hop albums. This is way too big. (B) will be too big, as well. For (A), she would have 48 hip hop albums—for a total of 60.

6. **B** To obtain the least possible value of q, you need to use the greatest possible value of p. If you are not sure about this, try out several values of p. When $p = 4$, $q = -52$. Take care not to select a negative p, as the cube p will also be negative and when you subtract that negative from $3p$, you will be adding.

HARD

7. **D** Plug in. If $x = 3$, then $6x + 9 = 27$, and $2x - 4 = 2$. The difference is 25. Plug 3 into the answer choices, and you get (D).

8. **C** Create a ratio box. For the actual total, use 180, as there are 180 degrees in a triangle. Your completed ratio box will look like this:

a	b	c	Total
2	3	4	9
20	20	20	20
40	60	80	180

9. **D** The easiest way to answer this question is to understand transformation of graphs. Just count how many units the graph moved. It moved 2 units to the right but did not move up or down. When a graph moves to the right, you need to subtract the number of units from x *inside* the parentheses.

10. **E** If you are comfortable manipulating equations with exponents, first isolate h by raising $h^{\frac{2}{3}}$ to the power of $\frac{3}{2}$. Having done so on the left side of the equation, you must do the same on the right side. Thus, we get: $h = k^3$. The question, however, asks for h^2, not x, so square both sides. As an alternative, you can plug in. To plug in here, it is useful to understand that $h^{\frac{2}{3}} = \sqrt[3]{h^2}$, as you will then pick an easy number, such as $h = 8$. In that case, the left side of the equation is 4, so $k^2 = 4$, and $k = 2$. As the question asks for h^2, our target answer is 16.

NOTES

NOTES

NOTES

NOTES

NOTES

NOTES

NOTES

NOTES

NOTES

Need More Than Math?

If you're looking to learn more about how to excel on the Math section of the SAT, you're in the right place. Our expertise extends far beyond math or the SAT. But this isn't about us, it's about getting you into the college of your choice.

One way to increase the number of acceptances you receive is to have strong test scores. So, if you're still experiencing some trepidation (Know what this means? Relax.), consider all your options.

We consistently improve students' scores through our books, classroom courses, private tutoring and online courses. Call 800-2Review or visit *PrincetonReview.com.*

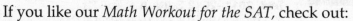